D0934511

EDGAR ALLAN POE,
A MYSTERY

EDGAR ALLAN POE

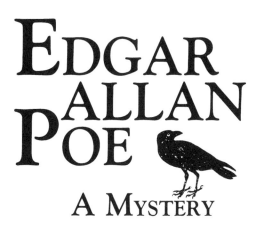

A MYSTERY

◆ BY ◆

MADELYN KLEIN ANDERSON

AN IMPACT BIOGRAPHY
FRANKLIN WATTS
NEW YORK ◆ CHICAGO ◆ LONDON ◆ TORONTO ◆ SYDNEY

Photographs courtesy of: Carl Glassman: p. 11; George Sullivan: pp. 13, 16; all other photographs are public domain.

Library of Congress Cataloging-in-Publication Data

Anderson, Madelyn Klein.
    Edgar Allan Poe : a mystery / by Madelyn Klein Anderson.
       p.   cm.—(An Impact biography)
    Includes bibliographical references and index.
    Summary: Chronicles the troubled life of the nineteenth-century
author, focusing on the haunting nature of his work.
    ISBN 0-531-13012-6 (lib. bdg.)—ISBN 0-531-15678-8 (pbk.)
    1. Poe, Edgar Allan, 1809–1849—Biography—Juvenile literature.
2. Authors, American—19th century—Biography—Juvenile literature.
[1. Poe, Edgar Allan, 1809–1849. 2. Authors, American.] I. Title.
PS2631.A79   1993
818'.309—dc20
   [B]   92-43935   CIP   AC

CONTENTS

The night is cold, dark, and still—the city will sleep for a few hours more until the weak winter sun rises and brings the streets to life. But where the dead sleep forever in the small cemetery, where silence and stillness are sacred, there is sound and movement. Shapeless shades, black on the black night sky, undulate over the looming gravestones—and disappear. The inevitable morning comes, and the old graveyard is silent and benign, belying the night's ghostly dance. But at the gravesite of Edgar Allan Poe, a half-empty bottle of brandy and three red roses speak of ghoulish celebration.

It is January 19, the anniversary of Poe's birth. And every year brings the same gesture of homage tainted by mockery, Poe's fate in death as in life. . . .

A Child
of Two Worlds
(1809–1826)

THEATRICAL COMMUNICATION.
*We congratulate the frequenters of the Theater
on the recovery of Mrs. Poe from her recent
confinement. . . . This charming little Actress
will make her reappearance Tomorrow Evening,
as* ROSAMUNDA, *in the popular play of*
ABAELLINO, *the* GREAT BANDIT, *a part
peculiarly adapted to her figure and talents.*
(*from the* Boston Gazette,
February 9, 1809)

The charming Mrs. Poe had barely recovered from
the birth of Edgar, her second son, when she was back
on the boards, not to please the public but to put
money into the Poe larder, for it was very bare.

Elizabeth Arnold Hopkins Poe and her husband,
David Poe, Jr., were repertory company actors. Elizabeth Arnold had gone onto the stage quite naturally.
She was a young child when she first performed with
her mother, a well-known actress in Wales and later in
the United States. But David Poe was no actor. He
had started out to be a lawyer but had given up his law
studies for the theater, considered a disreputable profession at the time. Possibly the actor's life appealed to

him, since he was a handsome young man. More probably, he had met and wanted to be near the charming
Elizabeth, despite the wedding ring placed on her fin-
ger by the company's talented comedian, a Mr. Hopkins. But as luck would have it, Elizabeth was soon the
young Widow Hopkins, and very soon after that, Mrs.
David Poe, Jr.

Elizabeth Poe was the star in the family and the
breadwinner. When she was incapacitated by preg-
nancy or illness, family finances suffered. Her husband
was given work largely as a favor to her. David Poe
drank, gambled, and had a hot temper that did not
endear him to the other players. Their marriage could
not handle the burden of two-year-old William Henry
Leonard (called simply Henry) and the newborn
Edgar. So as soon as they could leave Boston, the
family went to Baltimore to unburden themselves of
Henry, leaving him with his Poe grandparents or perhaps with friends—the record is unclear.

The Poe family had once been wealthy, but David
Poe, Sr.'s patriotism during the American Revolution
had impoverished them. Known as "General Poe," he
had been a major who served as assistant deputy quartermaster general for Baltimore, and he had used most of
his fortune to supply troops under the Marquis de Lafayette. General Poe was never repaid, which seemed
to matter little to him, for he served his country once
again in the defense of Baltimore against the British
during the War of 1812. The loss of that money, however, would matter a great deal to several of his seven
children and ultimately to his grandchildren, particularly Edgar Poe.

Not long after the visit to Baltimore, David Poe,
Jr. dropped out of sight of his contemporaries and of

history. Elizabeth Poe was to have yet another child, a daughter she named Rosalie, in December of 1810, but whether David was this child's father has always been open to conjecture. Elizabeth was fending for herself by this time, but in the summer of 1811, her health failed. Elizabeth Poe made her last stage appearance on October 11, 1811, in Richmond, Virginia. She was dying of consumption, at that time the socially acceptable name for tuberculosis, a disease that always carried a stigma. (This was so despite the fact that virtually everyone had the disease at one time or another, although often it did not progress beyond the initial infection.) It had become fashionable for the well-to-do ladies of Richmond to provide food and nursing to the sick and poor, and the charming actress and her two tiny children, Edgar and Rosalie, were well cared for in those last days.

Elizabeth Arnold Hopkins Poe died on December 8, 1811. She was twenty-four, or perhaps a few years older. She left Edgar a small watercolor portrait of herself and two small sketches she had drawn of Boston scenes. She noted on the back of one sketch how happy she had been in that city. Elizabeth also left him a packet of letters whose contents were never divulged. For Rosalie there was a box, meant for jewels in better times. Family tradition held that David Poe, Jr. died within days or weeks of Elizabeth's death, possibly in Norfolk, where Rosalie had been born.

Two of the women who had been caring for Elizabeth Poe and her children now each took a child into her home. This was a stroke of good luck, particularly since a catastrophic fire was to destroy the Richmond Theater only two weeks later, killing seventy-two people. This event left more orphans dependent on the

kindness of affluent families to rescue them from in-
stitutional care. (The adult Edgar Poe was to claim on
occasion that the fire had killed both his parents, probably because this explanation cast a more dramatic
light on his earliest days.) Edgar, who was almost
three, went to live with Mr. and Mrs. John Allan, and
the year-old Rosalie went to the home of Mr. and Mrs.
William Mackenzie. Both children were said to have
been baptized a few days or weeks later (although this
is not certain in Edgar's case) as Edgar Allan Poe and
Rosalie Mackenzie Poe, keeping their birth surnames
in the manner of the times. At some point, Rosalie
was legally adopted, but Edgar was not. Legal adoption
was not the custom then, and no one thought it mat-
tered. But Edgar was one day to suffer bitterly from this
lack of protection under the law.

Edgar's childhood with the Allans was idyllic.
The couple was well-off and had no children of their
own (although Mr. Allan had an illegitimate son).
Edgar was soon somewhat spoiled by his doting foster
mother, whom Edgar called "Ma," and her sister,
Nancy Valentine, a permanent member of the Allan
household. Edgar grew into "a lovely little fellow, with
dark curls and brilliant eyes, dressed like a young
prince . . . (who) . . . charmed everyone by his child-
ish grace, vivacity, and cleverness. His disposition was
frank, affectionate, and generous, and he was very
popular."[1]

When he turned five, Edgar was sent to a local
dame's school, a private school run by women with
whatever small education they might have picked up
from other dame's schools. The tuition was $4.00 quar-
terly. A year later, Mr. Allan enrolled both Edgar and
his illegitimate son, Edwin Collier, at a nearby board-

ing school. Edgar was only six years old, and it must have been hard for a young child with his history of loss to live away from home.

He was soon to live even farther away, for in June of that year, 1815, the Allans and Edgar were off to England. The embargo on British goods resulting from the War of 1812 had been lifted, and the English were demanding the American tobacco that had been in short supply during the war. Mr. Allan, whose firm, Ellis and Allan, dealt in tobacco and all kinds of other merchandise, foresaw good profits in setting up an overseas operation called Allan and Ellis.

The journey across the Atlantic took a nightmarish thirty-four days, and only Edgar, a good sailor, enjoyed it. It took the women a month to recuperate when they finally disembarked in Liverpool. The family visited Mr. Allan's sisters in Scotland, where little Edgar may have spent a short time at the Old Grammar School at Irvine. By October 1815, they had settled down in London, and early in 1816 Edgar was sent off to a boarding school across town under the tutelage of the Misses Dubourg (a name to turn up later in Poe's *The Murders in the Rue Morgue*). Mr. Allan paid an extra fee for Edgar to have his own bed, a luxury in English schools of the day.

But by 1818, the Allans were not doing so well. Frances Allan was constantly ailing, business was not good, and finances were a problem. John Allan wrote home to cut off the tuition for his son Edwin Collier, and Edgar was sent to the less expensive Manor House School in Stoke, Newington. Many years later, the headmaster of the school, Dr. Bransby (who was to figure in Poe's *William Wilson*), reminisced: "Edgar Allan [the name he knew him by] was a quick and clever boy and would have been a very good boy if he had not been spoilt by his parents, but they spoilt him, and allowed him an extravagant amount of pocket money, which enabled him to get into all manner of mischief—still I liked the boy—poor fellow, but his parents spoilt him."[2]

John Allan didn't seem to think so and wrote home that Edgar was "a very fine Boy and a good Scholer [sic]" who was "growing wonderfully . . . enjoyed a good reputation and is both willing and able to receive instruction."[3]

Business did not pick up at Allan and Ellis, and by October of 1819, John Allan was being dunned for the rent. He had to ask Ellis to send money so that the family could leave England. By the end of December, Ellis and Allan in Richmond and Allan and Ellis in London announced their suspension and their intention "by their efforts to pay their creditors."

It took some months for Allan to wind up his affairs, and it was not until June of 1820 that the family left England for home. They were forced to stop over in New York because of Frances Allan's bad health, but finally arrived in Richmond at the end of July. Until they could set up their own household, they stayed with the Ellises, who characterized them as being "a little Englishised." After five years in England, it would have been surprising if they had not been.

Edgar, by now almost twelve, was entered into yet another school. The headmaster, Joseph H. Clarke, was much later to remember him as being at the school for five years, but three years seems more likely considering when the other events in Edgar's life took place. He received an impressive classical education, reading Ovid, Caesar, Virgil, Cicero, and Horace in Latin and Xenophon and Homer in ancient Greek. English literature and writing were not neglected, and young Edgar began to show signs of his talent. Clarke reminisced in later years, "While the other boys wrote mere mechanical verses, Poe wrote genuine poetry: the boy was a born poet. . . . When he was ten [twelve] Mr. Allan came to me one day with a manuscript volume of verses, which he said Edgar had written, and which the little fellow wanted to have published. He asked my advice. . . . I told him that Edgar . . . possessed a great deal of self-esteem, and that it would be very injurious to the boy to allow him to be flattered and talked about as the author of a printed book at his age. . . . The verses, I remember, consisted chiefly of pieces addressed to the different little girls in Richmond."[4] Poe's choice of subjects for poetry and his self-esteem were not to change in later years, when he sent the many women around him adulatory poems—sometimes the same poem.

Edgar was fond of Professor Clarke. When Clarke moved to Baltimore, Edgar wrote him a farewell letter in Latin, and it was Edgar who was selected to write a class ode as a parting gift. Poe visited Clarke in later years when he was in Baltimore, and Clarke was one of the few friends at Poe's funeral.

Although Edgar got along with his classmates, he was not really popular. It was known that he was the son of two actors, and his parentage stigmatized him in the snobbish society of the day. The proud boy, now in his early teens, remained quiet and aloof, although he had two or three close friends.

One of those friends was Robert Craig Stanard,

who took Edgar home to meet his mother one day in the spring of 1823. Jane Stith Craig Stanard was gracious and warm, and seemed to understand so well all the things that were troubling the fourteen-year-old Edgar—his ever-increasing differences with John Allan, his foster mother who was loving but sick and ineffectual most of the time, his need to express himself, to be himself, to know himself. How often the boy met with Mrs. Stanard is unknown. Some biographers say they met only two or three times; others believe "numerous" times, but they certainly met often enough for the relationship to be extremely important to Poe. The first of Poe's great "To Helen" poems was written for Mrs. Stanard. (Poe often changed a woman's name if he wasn't fond of it, and Jane became Helen of Troy. Whether the poem was first written in Poe's adolescence is debated, although Poe maintained he wrote it then, endeavoring to prove his precocious talent. It was first published in 1831.)

Within a year of their meeting, Mrs. Stanard had a mental breakdown and then died of consumption. Poe was devastated by the death, which some biographers say he associated with the death of his mother. Whether Mrs. Stanard was a mother figure or an object of adolescent love, which seems more likely, Edgar Poe was turning from boy to man. This made for many problems with Mr. Allan, who was already stressed by his inability to make his business matters go as he wanted them and who now could not control a maturing Edgar. What was going wrong, we do not know; probably it was the all-too-common tension between a sensitive adolescent, independent in his thinking and chafing against his dependency in all other matters, and an unsympathetic, impatient adult. And Allan was an adult, moreover, who was becoming increasingly aware that he was not Edgar's father.

Allan wrote to Henry Poe, Edgar's older brother, possibly as he was going off to sea:

> *I have just seen your letter [inquiring why Edgar had not written] . . . and am much afflicted, that he has not written you. He has had little else to do for me he does nothing & seems quite miserable, sulky & ill-tempered to all the Family. How we have acted to produce this is beyond my conception—why I have put up so long with his conduct is little less wonderful. The boy possesses not a Spark of affection for us nor a particle of gratitude for all my care and kindness towards him. I have given him a much superior Education than ever I received myself. If Rosalie has to relie on any affection from him God in his mercy preserve her. . . . I must end this with a devout wish that God may yet bless him & you & that Success may crown all your endeavors & between you your poor Sister Rosalie may not suffer. At least She is half your Sister & God forbid my dear Henry that We should visit upon the living the Errors & frailties of the Dead. . . .*[5]

Allan seems here to be alluding to Rosalie having been fathered by someone other than Henry and Edgar's father, a slur against their mother that was bitterly resented by Edgar. Allan may, of course, have only meant that the two brothers each had half a share in Rosalie's welfare, not that she was their half-sister, but he was given to making such ambiguous statements about Rosalie's parentage. Since he had probably read the letters Elizabeth Poe left to Edgar, he may have had information on which to base his allusions.

Obviously, Edgar Allan Poe was having a difficult adolescence. He was constantly testing his powers. At about this time Edgar probably swam the James River for a distance of six miles (9.6 km) against the currents, a noteworthy feat about which he bragged his entire life.

Edgar was also reveling in the pride of being a Poe and not an Allan. The Marquis de Lafayette was making a triumphal tour of the United States and had inquired in Baltimore after General Poe. When told the General was dead (he had died in 1816 while Edgar was in England), Lafayette had visited his grave and, kneeling, said, "Ici repose un coeur noble!"— "Here lies a noble heart!" The next day Lafayette had visited the General's wife, Edgar's grandmother, and told her, "Your husband was my friend, and the aid I received from you both was greatly beneficial to me and my troops."[6] (Mrs. Poe had personally supervised the making of 500 pairs of trousers for the ill-clad soldiers under Lafayette's command.) Think how the heart of the young grandson must have swelled on hearing this, particularly in light of the thinly veiled contempt his fellows had for his actor-parents. And when Lafayette came to Richmond, Edgar Poe, then a lieutenant in the Junior Morgan Riflemen, was in the forefront of the honorary bodyguard chosen by Lafayette as his escort. Poe was sure that his troop was chosen because he was the grandson of General Poe. It was more likely that Lafayette was charmed by the very young troopers. The reason matters little, however—Poe's pride was glorious. But his conduct at home seemed to have been less so.

The difficulties at home were not resolved even after John Allan's financial woes came to an end with a large inheritance from his uncle. The Allans and Nancy Valentine were provided for handsomely, and Edgar must have relaxed in the knowledge that he would eventually inherit the Allan fortune. It never seems to have occurred to him that he had no legal claim on Allan and that he was there only on the man's sufferance, which was showing signs of wearing thin.

When he was sixteen, Edgar incurred more of Allan's wrath by declaring his love for a young lady of about fifteen who lived across the way from the Allans's imposing new house. She was Sarah Elmira Royster, and her father also objected to the relationship. Despite this, Edgar was an ardent suitor, and the couple were unofficially engaged when he went off to the University of Virginia at Charlottesville in February 1826. Although Edgar wrote Elmira frequently, her father intercepted the letters, and she thought she had been abandoned. Elmira was soon engaged—officially this time—to marry another. After all, she was close to sixteen by now, and waiting for Edgar Allan Poe might mean spinsterhood. (Poe's *Song*, which starts "I saw thee on thy wedding day," was written about her and published the year before she became Mrs. Elmira Royster Shelton.)

At seventeen, Poe had lost his mother, his beloved Mrs. Stanard, and his wife-to-be.

CAST OUT,
AND CASTING ABOUT
(1826–1831)

On the 14th day of February, 1826, Edgar Allan Poe was entered in the matriculation books of the University of Virginia at Charlottesville, the school of advanced learning started by Thomas Jefferson. He enrolled in the classes of two professors, one in the School of Ancient Languages (Greek and Latin) and the other in the School of Modern Languages (French, German, Italian, and Spanish), and attended classes six days a week from 7:30 to 9:30 in the morning. Tuition was $60, and Allan provided him with little more money than that. A week after he matriculated, Edgar was already in desperate financial need. He had to buy books, and he had to socialize with other young men whose families could afford to send them to the university. He wrote home for money.

Allan's response was speedy—and negative. Poe was shocked, particularly since the letter was couched "in terms of utmost abuse," as he pointed out in the letter he fired back to his foster father. He didn't doubt that money would be forthcoming. After all, Allan had wanted him to go to the university, and he had to understand the need for money beyond the tuition. So Edgar charged what he could and played at cards to earn spending money. But like so many other young men, he lost more than he won and then borrowed to cover his debts. He was confident that Mr. Allan, like other parents, would eventually take care of everything.

In December, the faculty of the university conducted an investigation into allegations that "outsiders"—professionals—were gambling and drinking with the students. Edgar Allan Poe was named to appear before the investigators, and he testified that he had no knowledge of such activities. That did not mean that Edgar didn't gamble. He did, and he seems to have been very bad at it: His friend, Thomas Ellis, said in a newspaper story many years later that Poe's gambling debts at the university amounted to $2,500. Another acquaintance remembered a $2,000 figure. Either amount would have been about five years' average income at the time and hardly seems credible. It might have been that Poe was, in his peculiar way, bragging about how much he owed. He wanted to be "one of the boys," and he often sought to impress people by exaggerating his exploits at drinking and gambling, trying to be the gay young blade.

In the December in which the investigation took place, Poe took his examinations, conducted by two former presidents of the United States, James Madison and James Monroe, as well as two lesser luminaries. Poe was listed as excelling at senior French and the ancient languages. William Wertenbaker, a librarian at the school, reminisced, "I often saw him in the Lecture room and in the Library, but never in the slightest degree under the influence of intoxicating liquors. Among the Professors he had the reputation of being a sober, quiet and orderly young man, and to them and the officers, his deportment was uniformly that of an intelligent and polished gentleman. Although his practice of gaming did escape detection, the hardihood, intemperance, and reckless wildness imputed to him by his Biographers, had he been guilty of them, must inevitably have come to the knowledge of the Faculty and met with merited punishment. The records of which I then, and am still, the custodian, attest that at no time during the session did he fall under the censure of the faculty."[1]

But by the new year, Edgar was gone from the University of Virginia. Although many biographers say that Poe was expelled from the university for gambling and wild carousing, this was not so. John Allan took him out of school. A furious Allan had gone to Charlottesville and had paid all of Edgar's debts that *he* thought should be paid. Gambling debts were not among them. And for some reason, he refused to pay a fifteen-dollar bill from a Charlottesville merchant. Since Edgar was only seventeen and not legally bound by any contractual agreements, and since he had no property of his own from which to take the money, the merchant contemplated putting Edgar in jail. Common sense seems to have prevailed, and the complaint was finally withdrawn after some heart-stopping threats. Poe always felt that had it not been for this incident, John Allan might have returned him to the University of Virginia. He never did understand the extent of Allan's rejection of him.

If Frances Allan or her sister, "Aunt" Nancy, interceded on Poe's behalf, it is not documented. Fond as they were of him, they might have attempted to do something. But "Ma," who was ill once again, and Nancy Valentine, who was in the Allan household at the sufferance of its master, were in no position to defy John Allan.

Edgar was put to work as a bookkeeper at Ellis and Allan, who were winding up their partnership at this time. The quarreling between foster father and son grew more acrimonious, until, on March 19, 1827, Edgar made the mistake of leaving the house. He simply walked out, without money or clothes, other than those he wore. Soon starving and out on the streets, Edgar was now in the position of having to contact Allan by letter to beg for help. He planned to leave Richmond and go to Boston on a coaster, a boat that transported coal up the coast. Perhaps Poe traveled as a crew member, because John Allan didn't send him any money.

Somehow Edgar did get to Baltimore at about this time, possibly at a stopover of the boat, although it would seem doubtful that as part of the crew he would have had time to make the several visits he reportedly made to his brother, Henry. Poe always said that after leaving the Allan household he went to Greece to fight for Greek independence, with a detour to Russia, and from there had been sent home by the American consul. Like the story of his parents' death in the Richmond Theater fire, this had a more dramatic ring to it than what he actually did.

What Poe really did was to go to Boston and then enlist in the United States Army, using the pseudonym Edgar A. Perry. Some biographers find it easier to credit Poe with a voyage to Greece and Russia than with joining the army—they see the army as less than congenial to a poet. Be that as it may, Edgar Poe did very well as a soldier. He was assigned to an artillery regiment at Fort Independence in Boston harbor, and he had a roof over his head, three meals a day, and plenty of leisure time in which to write.

A month or two after Poe had enlisted, a printer, Calvin F. S. Thomas, published a small paperbound book, *Tamerlane and Other Poems by a Bostonian.* The Bostonian was Edgar Poe, who was not loathe to take on Boston citizenship when it might further sales, although he preferred the identity of a southern gentleman from Richmond. Indeed, he had valid claims to both. "Tamerlane" was the first of only two epic poems that Poe was to write—he was to abjure lengthiness as unpoetic. The book also included "Song" (to Elmira Royster), "Dreams," "Visit of the Dead," "Spirits of the Dead," "Evening Star," "Imitation," "Stanzas" (regarded by many as the most difficult poem Poe ever wrote), "A Dream," "The Happiest Day," and "The Lake," considered the best of his early poems.

It was Poe's first book, and in the preface he wrote, "The greater part of the poems . . . were written in the year 1821–2, when the author had not completed his fourteenth [actually thirteenth] year." Perhaps fifty copies were printed. The book was not reviewed, although it was noted in two source books of American poetry. Only a few copies have survived, and its very existence was doubted for many years. (A single copy was auctioned in 1990 for several hundred thousand dollars.)

Surprisingly, the writings of Henry Poe, Edgar's brother, were appearing regularly at this time in magazines like *The Saturday Evening Post* and *North American.* Henry Poe wrote mostly travel pieces; he traveled a lot as a seaman, and he, rather than Edgar, probably visited Greece and Russia. He also wrote some poems and stories, including a piece based on Edgar's un-happy romance with Elmira Royster. (An acquain-tance of Henry's also used the romance as the plot of a three-part verse drama published at this time.) Henry also had the temerity to publish several of Edgar's pieces as his own. Their sister Rosalie also had two poems published in 1827, refuting later aspersions on her intelligence by Poe biographers. She was not well educated nor impelled to learn for herself, but neither were most young women in those days.

In early November of 1827, Poe's artillery battery was ordered to Charleston harbor in South Carolina. The trip from Massachusetts was not an easy one. On November 20th, *The Charleston Courier* printed this "card of thanks" from the battery:

> *The undersigned, officers of the 1st Regiment of Ar-tillery, in behalf of ourselves, families, and a detach-ment of men, tender to Captain George Webb, our most unfeigned thanks, for his kind attention to us while on board the Brig Waltham, on her passage from the harbor of Boston to Charleston, South Carolina; more especially for his nautical abilities, under Divine Providence, in extricating the vessel under his command, from most imminent danger, when drifting on a lee shore, off the shoals of Cape Cod, as well as good management during several severe gales of wind, while on our passage. Wishing him the like success under every peril and dan-ger. . . .[2]*

Poe was appointed "artificer," or company clerk, in May of 1828, but by December, he wanted to leave the army. He made a first move toward reconciliation with

John Allan, since a discharge was made contingent on his foster father's permission: ". . . at no period of my life, have I regarded myself with a deeper satisfaction. . . . I have been in the American army as long as suits my ends or my inclination, and it is now time that I should leave it . . . I made known my circumstances to Lieut. Howard who promised me my discharge solely upon reconciliation with yourself. . . . He has always been kind to me, and, in many respects reminds me forcibly of yourself. . . . I . . . am no longer a boy tossing about on the world without aim or consistency. . . . My dearest love to Ma."[3]

Poe's artillery battery was soon on the move again, off to Fortress Monroe in Virginia, where Poe was again put on desk duty, this time in the adjutant's office. Not long afterward, Poe wrote to Allan, exulting in the fact that he had met the commanding officer of the regiment, who had known his grandfather General Poe and also knew the Allans. The commanding officer had assured Poe of his discharge immediately upon receiving Allan's consent. However, Poe would also need a replacement, someone who would volunteer in his place so that the army would not be out a man.

Poe decided to write to John Mackenzie, his friend and Rosalie's foster brother, asking him to use his influence with John Allan for help in a broader scheme—not only to get him out of the regiment, but also to get him back in the army again as an appointee to the United States Military Academy at West Point. Officer status—barring warfare—meant security, income, and social standing.

"Richmond and the United States were too narrow a sphere and the world shall be my theatre," the young man exulted. He was sure of success at West Point, based on his successful experience as an enlisted man. In January 1829, Poe became regimental sergeant major, the top enlisted man of the unit. This was a title, not a rank, just as his grandfather had the title of quartermaster general but the rank of major. Unfortunately, rank, not title, determined pay grades, and Edgar was as poor as ever.

Poe's foster family, however, was relieved to think of him as settled. Even John Allan relaxed his disapprobation. Unfortunately, Poe's "Ma" had little time to savor his new position—she died the following month. Although Frances Allan had asked her husband on her deathbed not to bury her until Edgar arrived home on leave, Allan disregarded her wishes. Poe was too late by only a few hours to see his beloved "Ma" for the last time, adding to his distress. But Allan was cordial enough in welcoming him back and saw that Poe had proper mourning clothes. He also agreed to give his consent to a discharge and contacted powerful friends about a West Point appointment for Edgar.

Poe returned to Fortress Monroe and arranged for the necessary substitute to replace him, a sergeant who was going to reenlist anyway and was willing—for $75, well over the going rate of $12—to specify that he was a substitute for Perry/Poe. Poe was too anxious to get out to wait for better terms. The deal was made, and he was discharged on the 15th of April, 1829. His commanding officer wrote a letter of recommendation, saying ". . . his conduct was unexceptionable—he at once performed the duties of company clerk and assistant in the Subsistent Department, both of which duties were promptly and faithfully done. His habits are good, and entirely free from drinking."[4] Poe also received the endorsements of the adjutant and the commanding officer of Fortress Monroe. These recommendations, plus letters from influential members of the United States Congress, including the Speaker of the House, were brought directly to the Secretary of War, John H. Eaton, in Washington. But the appointment process to West Point was a lengthy one, and Poe was now out of a job.

He was living in Baltimore, possibly with a cousin, Mrs. Beacham, or at the home of his father's sister, Maria Poe Clemm. He wrote to Allan that he was meeting "gentlemen of high standing" in the city. John Allan responded positively to this letter, sending Poe a bank check for one hundred dollars to keep him going.

With Allan's intercession on his behalf and money in his pocket, Poe became confident of his foster father's continued support. He had written "Al Aaraaf," the longest and one of the most difficult of his poems, and the publishers Carey, Lea, and Carey said they would print it—if John Allan would guarantee to make up any loss they might incur if it didn't sell. Would he? He would not. To make matters worse, Poe had to ask Allan once again for money to live on. Fifty dollars of the one hundred Allan had sent had gone to Poe's army replacement. His second cousin Edward Mosher had stolen $16 from Poe's pocket while he slept, and Poe had only been able to retrieve $10 when he in turn rifled his cousin's pockets.

Allan had undoubtedly thought that calls upon his pocketbook like this were over. He was annoyed and mistrustful and intimated to Poe that he need not think of coming back home to Richmond, but he did send money. Poe was disconcerted by Allan's antagonism and wrote several letters carefully detailing his expenditures so that Allan would not think him improvident. And when Poe decided to go to Washington personally to see what was holding up his appointment to West Point, he walked the entire way from Baltimore and back rather than use the money for carfare. Poe did see Secretary of War Eaton (government officials were far more accessible in those days!), only to be told he would have to wait his turn on the list. His turn was not to come until the following year.

Meanwhile, Poe concentrated on his poetry. He sent a copy of some poems to John Neal, an editor-novelist-critic-lawyer, who responded in the "To Correspondents" column of *Yankee; and Boston Literary Gazette* (sic) for September 1829: "If E.A.P. of Baltimore—whose lines about *Heaven,* though he professes to regard them as altogether superior to any thing in the whole range of American poetry, save two or three trifles referred to, are, though nonsense, rather exquisite nonsense—would but do himself justice, he might make a beautiful and perhaps a magnificent poem. There is a good deal here to justify such a hope. . . ."[5] Praise from a man known as the great autocrat of critics! Poe was ecstatic.

His second volume of poems, *Al Aaraaf, Tamerlane & Minor Poems,* was published by Hatch & Dunning toward the end of 1829, apparently without a guarantee, and he sent Neal a copy for review. He enclosed a letter: "I am young—not yet twenty [he was not yet twenty-one]—*Am* a poet—if deep worship of all beauty can make me one . . . I am about to publish a volume of 'Poems'—the greater part written before I was 15."[6] In December, Neal published passages from the poems along with an appreciation of Poe's potential. Poe's precocity was not an issue despite his claim for consideration on that basis, and the poems received mixed, mostly bad, reviews.

Then, in March of 1830, the long-awaited appointment to the Military Academy arrived. Poe was now twenty-one, but Military Academy records show him to be nineteen years and five months old as of July 1, 1830, the date he first appeared on the muster rolls at the academy. The year and a half was undoubtedly shaved off to allow the now over-age Poe to be enrolled. As a "minor," he needed Allan's consent to enter the corps, but Allan did not balk at signing the necessary papers. He also provided Poe with four blankets, some handkerchiefs, and a twenty-dollar bank check that would reach Poe a month later at West Point. As usual with Allan, what seemed like a lot of money was nowhere near enough to keep Poe going. And even that little trickle of support would soon dry up.

Poe was discontented at the Military Academy. Perhaps it was his taste for literary life—a new poem, "Sonnet—To Science," appeared in two magazines as he started classes—or the fact that he was not prepared for the differences between the discipline of the academy and the relative freedom he had enjoyed as an enlisted man. Poe was a little older than the rest of the plebes, and his experience made them stand somewhat in awe of him. He had no compunction about enhancing that awe with stories of having gone to Russia and to Greece during its war of independence, and he did nothing to squelch the rumor that his mother had been the illegitimate daughter of Benedict Arnold. Perhaps Poe himself had planted the rumor, or perhaps he wanted to believe it himself. He had written a letter to Allan while visiting the Poe family in Baltimore, saying, "I have learned . . . that I am the grandson of General Benedict Arnold." The staunchly patriotic Poes might have thought they were shaming Edgar's actress-mother further by telling her son this, if indeed they had, but again Edgar might have chosen to use this romantic notion to bolster his image.

Poe was inclined to romanticize reality and showed little sense in dealing with real relationships. He owed additional money to the sergeant who had acted as his substitute, and the sergeant had written to Allan to get it. Allan replied that Poe had already sent the money to the sergeant via another soldier. This was not so, and this misconception represented a threat to the soldier's safety when he could not produce the money. When Poe found out, he immediately wrote to the sergeant. But he wrote in the heat of anger, not only at the misrepresentation but because of a recent instance of Allan's abuse of his family—probably another snide remark about Rosalie's parentage. Childishly, Poe wrote that "Mr. A. is not very often sober—which accounts for [this confusion]." The sergeant is said to have told this to Allan, who, understandably, was furious. According to his standards, Allan had been more than generous with Edgar Poe. According to Poe, Allan had not lived up to the tacit bargain he had made when taking Edgar into his family.

Allan didn't recognize any such bargain or obligation. Since Edgar was not blood kin and was not adopted, Allan did not look upon Edgar as his heir. Allan, by now fifty-one and the father of two more illegitimate sons (twins) by yet another married woman, had decided to remarry. He had proposed to Nancy Valentine, his wife's sister. It is said that Poe talked her out of the marriage. But it is more likely that Allan realized that a younger woman could give him a legitimate heir. In due time, the rich young wife he chose, Louisa Patterson, provided him with three heirs, all sons. And Poe, who never could understand how the man he had regarded all his life as his father could cast him aside, finally realized the relationship was over.

Without money from Allan, Poe could not afford to stay at the Academy. Without permission from Allan, he could not resign from the Academy. Since neither were forthcoming from Allan, Poe wrote him a letter of recrimination, threatening to neglect all studies and duties until he was dismissed, which would be a disgrace to the family. Allan did not bother to answer, but he annotated the letter for filing: "I do not think the Boy has one good quality. He may do or act as he pleases, tho' I wd have saved him but on his own terms & conditions since I cannot believe a word he writes."[7]

Poe made good his threat and was brought up before a court-martial for neglect of duty and disobedience to orders. He had been absent from parades and roll calls and refused to attend church when ordered to do so by the officer of the day on the 23rd of January, 1831. He also refused to attend classes on the 25th. Poe pleaded not guilty to the absences from the parades and roll calls, but guilty to the other charges and was dismissed from the service of the United States. He was not dismissed for drunkenness or rowdyism, as is often alleged. Nor was he thrown out for poor scholastic performance; in a class of eighty-seven, he ranked seventeenth in mathematics and third in French.

So little did Poe feel any onus connected with his court-martial and dismissal from the service that four days after his dismissal became official on March 6, he wrote to Colonel Sylvanus Thayer, superintendent of the Academy, "I intend by the first opportunity to proceed to Paris with the view of obtaining, thro' the interest of the Marquis de La Fayette, an appointment (if possible) in the Polish Army. . . . The object of this letter is . . . to request that you give me such assistance as may lie in your power in furtherance of my views. A certificate of 'standing' in my class is all that I have any right to expect. Any thing farther—a letter to a friend in Paris—or to the Marquis—would be a kindness which I should never forget."[8] There is no record of an answer, and what Poe had in mind is difficult to see, other than that it is the kind of fantasy he enjoyed indulging in.

In fact, the Academy seemed to bear him no ill will. Poe was given official permission to solicit subscriptions from the cadets for a book called simply *Poems*. One hundred and thirty-one cadets (of 232) signed up for a copy, and the price, $1.25, was withheld from their pay. Most were none too happy when they received their purchase. The book was badly printed on poor paper and cheaply bound in an ugly cover. The cadets considered some of the poems so bad that they joked about them. They were not aware that they had two new masterpieces in their hands—a revised "To Helen" and "Israfel"—along with poems that presaged Poe's belief that the most important theme of a poet was "the great imagined landscape": "The City in the Sea," "Al Aaraaf," and "Fairy Land."

Poe was to receive a check from the Military Academy for $170, more than he was to make from his poetry in times to come.

Poe knew his work was good, and he knew his potential for greatness. He left West Point about two weeks after the court-martial and headed to nearby New York City to conquer the literary world.

WRITER AND EDITOR, SUITOR AND HUSBAND (1831–1837)

Poe's arrival in New York City in February 1831 was inauspicious. He had a chest cold, a cough, a violent and constant headache, and a bloody discharge from his ear. He knew no one, and he had no money. Once again he wrote to John Allan, pleading, "I have no money—no friends—I have written to my brother—but he cannot help me. . . . I hardly know what I am writing—I will write no more—Please send me a little money—quickly—and forget what I said about you."[1] There is no record of an answer.

Somehow Edgar survived; perhaps the check from the Military Academy reached him. But by early May, he was back in Baltimore. He moved in with his widowed aunt, Maria Poe Clemm, and her children, Henry and Virginia. His Grandmother Poe, Mrs. Clemm's mother, was also living there, as was his brother Henry. Mrs. Poe's government pension of $240 a year helped support them all. Mrs. Clemm's remarkable capacity for caring for her brood marks her as probably the saintliest character or most tenacious beggar in all literary biography. It couldn't have been easy. Her mother was paralyzed by a stroke, and her nephew, the twenty-four-year-old Henry Poe, was dying of tuberculosis—he would be dead just a few months later. Very little is known about Mrs. Clemm's son Henry, who was about fifteen when Edgar Poe moved in. (There is a tendency to confuse Henry Clemm with Henry Poe, and both Henrys are said to have gone to sea, been drunkards, and died young.) The only bright spot in the household was Poe's rousing, cheerful, playful, pretty little cousin, Virginia Eliza. Poe tutored her and acted as her confidante and companion, and Virginia idolized him and carried his messages to his young lady friends.

Poe was carrying on several brief romances, one with a cousin, Elizabeth Herring—the recipient of one of his "To Elizabeth" poems. It is thought, too, that his relationship with a young woman named Mary Starr started at this time. Sometimes also known as Mary Devereaux because Devereaux was the name of the uncle with whom she lived, Mary Starr was to figure in Poe's later years. However, their early relationship was quickly ended. Fathers and uncles were none too pleased to have a penniless Poe come courting.

When Henry Poe died, Edgar Poe inherited nothing from him but a debt of eighty dollars. His only hope of discharging the debt was to get the money from Allan. Once again he wrote begging for money. In his letter he said that he had been arrested for the debt, but this was probably put in for effect, as he was wont to do. While Poe did face arrest, there is no documentation of his actually having been jailed. Allan might have left him to that sorry fate were it not for a follow-up letter from Mrs. Clemm that persuaded Allan to ask one of his business agents to pay the debt and give Poe an additional twenty dollars. But out of meanness or just plain oversight, Allan neglected to mail the letter of authorization for over a month, by which time Poe was begging: "For the sake of the love you bore me when I sat upon your knee and called you father do not forsake me this only time."[2]

Poe could not stretch that twenty dollars as far as it needed to go, but at least the threat of jail was removed. He was beginning to see his work published. Poe had turned to writing short stories now, like "Berenice" and "Morella." He could turn these out more quickly than his poems, and so raise more money. And poetry required more peace of mind to write than he had at the time. He did, however, write one of his great love poems, "To One in Paradise." Its theme was one that Poe considered the most sublime, the most tragic: the death of a beautiful woman.

In the summer of 1831, Poe submitted five stories to a contest sponsored by the *Saturday Courier* in Philadelphia. He didn't win, but the journal published the stories—"Metzengerstein," "The Duc de L'Omelette" (a satire), "A Tale of Jerusalem," "A Decided Loss" (later titled "Loss of Breath"), and "The Bargain Lost" (a draft for his later "Bon-Bon")—in successive issues, making his name more familiar to the public. Whether Poe was paid is unknown, and doubtful. Failed contest winners were fair game—not having to pay the entrants any fees made up for the prize money publishers had to lay out. (Considering that such contests also raised money by drawing in new subscribers, it's a wonder there weren't more of them.)

Poe was also being published in *The Minerva* and *The Saturday Visiter* in Baltimore and *The Literary Gazette* in Albany as well as the *Saturday Courier*. His poems were being reviewed in *The New York Mirror*,

The New York Enquirer, and elsewhere. Even so, at the usual one dollar a page paid for stories, his output brought in very little.

If not winning fortune, Poe was achieving a certain amount of fame. In October 1833, he won the first prize of fifty dollars in a short story contest run by *The Saturday Visiter* for his "Manuscript Found in a Bottle," one story in the collection Poe called *Tales of the Folio Club.* The judges announced that they had had difficulty in choosing the winning story, since stylistically they were all so new and so engrossing. *The Saturday Visiter* had also offered a twenty-five-dollar poetry prize, and Poe had entered his "Coliseum." He did not win the prize because, as it later turned out, the judges did not want to give both prizes to the same person. An editor at *The Saturday Visiter,* writing under a pseudonym, was given the poetry prize instead. When Poe found out, he was furious, and he took action. The winner, John Hill Hewitt, reminisced many years later (1877):

> . . . I encountered Mr. Poe. He approached me with an ominous scowl on his features. "You have used underhanded means, sir, to obtain that prize over me," said he, sternly. "I deny it, sir," was my reply. "Then why did you keep back your real name?" "I had my reasons, and you have no right to question me." "But you tampered with the committee, sir." "The committee are gentlemen above being tampered with, sir; and if you say that you insult them," I replied, looking him full in the face. "I agree that the committee are gentlemen," replied he, his dark eyes flashing with anger, "but I cannot place you in that category." My blood mounted up to

fever heat in a moment, and with my usual impul-
siveness, I dealt him a blow which staggered him, for
I was physically his superior. There was every pros-
pect of a very pretty fight, for Poe was full of pluck,
but several gentlemen, friends to both parties, inter-
fered, and the affair was "nipped in the bud." There
was no duel—much to the disappointment of our
friends and well-wishers.[3]

Writing under a pseudonym was not cheating; Poe himself often did it. But his characteristic bellicosity was aroused by being deprived of what he thought was his due. He needed the money, and he was not a good sport—he hated being bested. This absolute surety of his own superiority would infuriate many people be-sides Hewitt over the years.

One of the judges of the contest, John Pendleton Kennedy, a novelist and later a United States con-gressman, befriended Poe. Kennedy offered him money and the loan of a horse for transportation. He also found Poe several small editorial and writing jobs. Kennedy tried, unsuccessfully, to interest his own pub-lishers, Carey & Lea, in publishing *Tales of the Folio Club*. When Kennedy wrote to them of Poe's dire need for money, the publishers did go so far as to act on his behalf and sell one of the tales to an annual magazine at a dollar a page, reserving the right to publish the story in book form if it got good reviews. The book was never published, although the reviews of "Manuscript Found in a Bottle" were uniformly good.

In April of 1833, at still another low ebb, Poe again begged John Allan for help: "It has now been more than two years since you have assisted me, and more than three since you have spoken to me . . .

without friends, without any means, consequently of obtaining employment, I am perishing—absolutely perishing for want of aid. And yet I am not idle—nor addicted to any vice—nor have I committed any offence against society which would render me deserving of so hard a fate. For God's sake pity me, and save me from destruction."

For a man with the sensitivity of Edgar Poe, this must have been difficult to write—unless it was the writer writing and not the man. Allan made him no response. He simply noted on Poe's letter: "Apl 12, 1833: it is now upwards of 2 years since I received the above precious relict of the Blackest Heart and deepest ingratitude alike destitute of honour and principle [.] Every day of his life has only served to confirm his debased nature—Suffice it to say my only regret is in Pity for his failing—his Talents are of an order that can never prove a comfort to their possessor."[4]

Allan never recognized the meanness of his own role in their relationship; he failed to understand that his sudden withdrawal of support, both financial and familial, from an adolescent and completely dependent boy lay at the root of the problem. Mercifully, for the Allan letters are painful to read, this was to be the last letter Poe was to write his foster father. He was, however, supposed to have visited Allan a year later for the last time, when he heard of Allan's serious illness. Much has been made of this visit, and there are a number of versions of it, depending on whether they came from Poe's friend or foe. The worst version was that Poe forced his way into Allan's house, where he demanded his old room back, reviled the second Mrs. Allan and her child, and fled when he heard

Allan coming. The most favorable version says that Poe stayed with the Allans as a guest.

Neither of these scenarios ring true. Somewhat more credible is the account offered by Thomas Ellis, the son of Allan's partner and a friend of Poe's, although he was recounting an incident that had happened almost fifty years before and that he knew about only from hearsay:

> *A short time previous to Mr. Allan's death, on the 27th of March, 1834, . . . Mrs. Allan . . . hearing the front doorbell ring . . . opened the door herself. A man of remarkable appearance stood there, & without giving his name asked if he could see Mr. Allan. She replied that Mr. Allan's condition was such that his physicians had prohibited any person from seeing him except his nurses. The man was Edgar A. Poe, who was, of course, perfectly familiar with the house. Thrusting her aside and without noticing her reply, he passed rapidly upstairs to Mr. Allan's chamber, followed by Mrs. Allan. As soon as he entered the chamber, Mr. Allan raised his cane, & threatening to strike him if he came within his reach, ordered him out; upon which Poe withdrew, & that was the last time they ever met.*[5]

That is, if the incident ever took place at all. A month later, March 1834, John Allan was dead. Poe's last shred of hope that he might have been remembered in Allan's will was soon shattered.

His friend and mentor, John Pendleton Kennedy, used his influence in getting Poe published in a new magazine he was interested in, *The Southern Literary*

Messenger. The venture was also supported by other men of distinction, including Washington Irving, James Fenimore Cooper, John Quincy Adams, and Chief Justice of the Supreme Court, John Marshall, all men who wanted the South to have a more important place in the literary world. In 1835, Poe contributed several pieces to the *Messenger,* including "Hans Pfaall," a send-up of balloon flights, a very popular subject of the time. The story was a pioneer contribution to the genre of science fiction. Poe enhanced his story with so many scientific details that it seemed absolutely feasible. He was to write a number of such science fiction pieces and present them as absolute truth. They were hoaxes that fooled hundreds of thousands of people.

Poe's writings for *The Southern Literary Messenger* and other journals were drawing in small amounts of money that, added to Grandmother Poe's pension, made the household somewhat more comfortable, but only for a short while. General Poe's widow died on July 7, 1835, at the age of seventy-nine, and the government pension died with her. Poe was in dire need of more income to care for Mrs. Clemm and Virginia— there was no question in his mind of abandoning his aunt and cousin. Kennedy encouraged him to go to Richmond to *The Southern Literary Messenger* and its editor, Thomas Willis White.

Poe was off to Richmond, where White gave him a job as an editorial assistant at $520 a year. Poe also tried to get an appointment as a professor of English at the Richmond Academy, but nothing came of his attempts. He may have become engaged to Elizabeth White, his employer's daughter, but nothing came of that, either. The story goes that Mr. White had accepted the engagement only if Poe didn't drink, a habit in which he seems to have indulged at this time, for reasons unknown. Perhaps it was because he was lonely or had too many bad thoughts about the difference in his circumstances from his early sheltered days in Richmond, or perhaps he just wanted to be sociable.

For whatever reasons Poe drank, he shouldn't have, for he could not hold his liquor—sometimes one drink was one too many. Why this was so has been a matter of conjecture for many years, and signs point to some organic or metabolic dysfunction. Whatever the etiology, the results could be horrendous. John W. Fergusson, a printer and messenger boy at *The Messenger*, reminisced: "Mr. Poe was a fine gentleman when he was sober. He was ever kind and courtly, and at such times every one liked him. But when he was drinking he was about one of the most disagreeable men I have ever met."[6]

Poe stopped drinking, but nothing came of his romance with Elizabeth White, for at this time galling news came from Baltimore. Mrs. Clemm wrote that Neilson Poe, husband to one of Mrs. Clemm's stepdaughters (and second cousin to Edgar), had contacted her on behalf of his wife, who was concerned for the welfare of her stepsister, Virginia. Neilson had offered to become Virginia's guardian and assist Mrs. Clemm financially as well.

Poe was devastated at the thought of losing "Muddy" and "Sis," as mother and daughter were called. Virginia was thirteen, more than a child but less than a woman. (Mrs. Clemm was later to insist that Virginia was fifteen. This discrepancy may have been due to forgetfulness or to confusion over the fact that Mrs. Clemm is said to have had yet another daughter named Virginia Sarah or Virginia Maria, who died at the age of two on the same day that the second Virginia—Virginia Eliza—was baptized.)

Until now, Poe had probably not thought of Virginia as a candidate for wife. Now he wrote to Mrs. Clemm:

> *I have no desire to live and will not. . . . I love, you know I love Virginia passionately devotedly. . . . All my thoughts are occupied with the supposition that both you & she will prefer to go with N. Poe. . . . It is useless to disguise the truth that when Virginia goes with N. P. that I shall never behold her again. . . . I had procured a sweet little house in a retired situation on church hill—newly done up and with a large garden and every convenience—at only $5 per month. . . . [I am] Among strangers with not one soul to love me. . . . White has engaged to make my salary $60 a month. . . . She will have far—very far better opportunities of entering into society here than with N. P. Every one here receives me with open arms.*

And in a postscript: "For Virginia, My love, my own sweetest Sissy, my darling little wifey, think well before you break the heart of your cousin, Eddy. . . . Dearest Aunty consider my happiness while you are thinking about your own."[7]

While they were thinking about it—which some say was not very long, since Mrs. Clemm might have stage-managed the whole crisis—their Eddy was in trouble. He drank and had attacks of depression, perhaps in the reverse order. White spoke of Poe being "the victim of melancholy. I should not be at all astonished to hear that he has been guilty of suicide."[8] Mr. Kennedy wrote to Poe, "It is strange that just at the time when every body is praising you and when Fortune has begun to smile upon your hitherto wretched circumstances you should be invaded by these villainous blue devils."[9]

Neither the blue devils nor drinking interfered seriously with Poe's work. He was a great asset to the *Messenger*, and despite Mr. White's protestations that he was a mere assistant, Poe actually did most of the work and was responsible for a gigantic leap in circulation. Readers enjoyed his short stories, his poetry (it was an age in which reading poetry aloud was a favored entertainment), and his articles. But Poe soon left White's employ and returned to Baltimore. Perhaps he was fired for drunkenness, as many people have said; it is more likely that he left to see to Mrs. Clemm and Virginia.

On September 22, 1835, in Baltimore, Edgar Poe and Virginia Clemm took out a license to be married. They may have gone through a marriage ceremony, and many years later Mrs. Clemm said they had, but there is no record of it. And when Poe brought Virginia and Mrs. Clemm back to Richmond in early October, the women set up their own separate residence. Eight months later, on May 16, 1836, Virginia and Edgar definitely went through a wedding ceremony, attended by friends, including Mr. White, who had rehired Poe, and his daughter Elizabeth, who apparently bore Poe no animosity. Poe was twenty-seven, and his new wife was just short of fourteen, or possibly sixteen.

A great deal of fuss has been made over Virginia's age, but in those days early marriage was commonplace. The more favored age for a young lady was sixteen, but brides of thirteen and fourteen were not uncommon, particularly among the poor. It was an advantageous way for parents or guardians to unburden themselves of an extra mouth to feed, and a young man needed a wife to cook and clean and keep him healthy sexually.

It has been conjectured that the marriage was never consummated—that Poe was celibate and Virginia a virgin during their life together. The famous psychoanalyst Maria Bonaparte did a psychoanalytic study (posthumous, of course) of Poe—with a preface by her mentor, Sigmund Freud—in which she theorized not only celibacy but a castration complex and necrophilia. Her theories are no longer seriously entertained. Although the lack of children made the celibacy theory difficult to disprove, it was easy to prove that both Edgar and Virginia had passionate temperaments; a neighbor had seen Virginia kiss Poe one day in Baltimore, and the neighbor recorded her shock at the abandon the girl displayed. And although Virginia was young when she married, she did grow older. Poe, too, wrote a friend that the first two years of their marriage had more of play than passion in it—the inevitable conclusion being that the reverse was true afterward. Nothing in Poe's romancing of the many women in his life would suggest that he was incapable of feeling passion or that he did not love his wife sexually.

Whatever their private life, about which Poe spoke little, it was publicly well known that Poe adored his laughing, beautiful young wife and that their marriage was a happy one. The presence of Mrs. Clemm was a bonus rather than a nuisance, for she kept Virginia company, fed Poe innumerable cups of the coffee he loved while he worked, soothed his aching brow when he could not sleep, and exercised her talents as housekeeper and cook. She managed their money beyond all reasonable expectations, something that at least in the beginning Virginia would probably not have done as well. She and Virginia gardened and sewed, sometimes earning extra money with their needles. The two women created an ambiance spoken of by all who visited them as poor but exceedingly attractive and scrupulously neat and clean.

Poe's literary output was increasing now. He even attempted a play, "Politian," then decided he didn't like it. He published five scenes for fillers in *The Southern Literary Messenger* and decided to print no more. Perhaps his newly honed talents as a reviewer made him aware of its flaws.

Poe had a genius for literary criticism. Although he elicited many a protest for his severity and occasionally his pedantry—Poe liked showing off his extensive knowledge, and others liked to denigrate it—he brought a new approach to literary reviews: honesty. At the time Poe wrote, reviews were used like advertisements to inflate the value of a work so it would draw readers. Poe was not above this sort of writing on occasion to accommodate a friend or repay a favor, but for the most part he wielded a wicked pen when he thought it was warranted. This did not inspire affection, and many victims sought to retaliate. They ridiculed everything about Poe: his works, his appearance, his character, his erudition, and his genius. The poet James Russell Lowell was to say that Poe was "three-fifths genius and two-fifths sheer fudge," but that was when Lowell was mad at him. Poe did fudge a little about his age and his personal history now and then, and he was often pompous in his literary judgments—but he was still a genius.

Poe's standards were high, and he came down hard on those who did not meet them, or on those whose work he simply did not like. He hammered away venomously at Henry Wadsworth Longfellow over the years; on the other hand, he was overly gentle and condescending with women writers. He was arrogant in his judgments, particularly about what he called "plagiarism," which was usually nothing more than a similarity in phrasing or theme. Poe himself was to be accused of such plagiarism. He simply dismissed the charges with contempt and continued his attacks on others. For himself, he demanded perfection. He revised his works over and over again, before and after they were published, seeking a better word here, a more rhythmic line there, and sometimes slashing and rebuilding with minute care.

Poe's fame was growing to the point that the Franklin Literary Society of Jefferson College, Pennsylvania, made him an honorary member in 1836. Yet he still could not get his stories published in book form. A friend of White's took the manuscript of a proposed collection to Harpers in New York, but the publisher declined it on the grounds that the stories had all been in print already and were somewhat too obscure. The editors did say that they would consider new stories or, better still, a full-length book. Poe was far too busy for that.

Poe was running the *Messenger* now as well as contributing to it. White's wife was dying of cancer, and he had little time for the magazine. Her illness was also costly, and White often had to borrow small sums to keep the magazine going. Poe was busy soliciting subscriptions, corresponding with writers and arranging to publish them (otherwise he would have to fill the pages himself), seeing to bills, overseeing the printing process, editing, and reviewing. His editorial influence on the literary world had grown far beyond anything White had achieved, much to the latter's chagrin. Nor did Poe get any extra money for all he did. White thought the salary he paid Poe, now $1,040 a year, more than adequate. In actuality, as Poe's workload increased, he was actually losing income because he had little time left to write the pieces that brought him extra money.

Poe seems to have occasionally indulged in drink during this period, although he could not possibly have done so to the extent his early biographers claimed, for he would never have been able to carry on his work as well as he did. At one point, however, Poe was disabled for some days with an unnamed illness that may have resulted from drinking. Poe always insisted that it was the other way around, that he became ill first and drank to make himself feel better. Then he took laudanum, an opium derivative and the cure-all of the day for everything from headaches to stomachaches to teething, to relieve the distress of the drinking. Nothing in Poe's behavior points to addiction to or dependence on laudanum, although his detractors trundle out some instances of his having begged for laudanum. That Poe probably used it to alleviate some ache or pain does not fit their theory that opium dreams were responsible for the strange and wondrous landscapes and images in Poe's works—as if a fertile imagination were not enough.

The cause of Poe's recurrent periods of prostration has not seriously been explored by modern medical practitioners. His illness has always been explained as drunkenness, even though it was a condition that could be induced by one drink. Poe may have been allergic to alcohol and to laudanum, or he may have already had the brain lesion his doctors were to diagnose in his later years. The kind of brain lesion Poe had would take the expertise of today's neurologists to diagnose. It is thought by some that Poe might also have been diabetic, and that alcohol could have thrown him into a semi- or fully comatose state.

Whatever the illness, it may have been responsible for Poe's leaving *The Southern Literary Messenger* for less arduous work or for the time to write a novel. Or White could have fired him, which he liked to imply: "Mr. Poe retired from the editorship of my work on the 3d instant [January 1837]. I am once more at the head of my affairs."[10] In another letter, White wrote, ". . . the *Messenger* is safe. It shall live—and it shall outlive all the injury it has sustained from Mr. Poe's management."[11] White did not specify the injuries. He may have thought that Poe's acerbic reviews would lose him customers or writers whose reputations belied Poe's condemnation. Several editors and publishers had accused Poe of vanity; some had called for Poe's dismissal. *The Newbern Spectator,* for example, said in its December 1836 issue, "We have been endeavouring for twelve months to convince the Editor of the Messenger [Poe] that his course was erroneous, discreditable to the South, promotive of bad taste, and ruinous to Mr. White's laudable enterprise. . . ."[12]

While Mr. White probably agreed, he defended his publication and his editor in a front-page editorial exonerating Poe from these charges, and he included laudatory statements from other journals about Poe's reviews. Although his exoneration was more a matter of good journalism than personal feeling, White could not legitimately complain about Poe's performance: the subscription list of *The Southern Literary Messenger* had expanded from 700 to 5,000 readers during the two years that Poe was filling its pages and acting as its unofficial editor. Poe's written contributions were clearly demonstrated in the January 1837 issue, the first for which he was not on staff and writing more or less anonymously. It contained two poems, four articles, and the first part of Poe's only novel, *The Narrative of Arthur Gordon Pym*.

The Narrative was science fiction presented as nonfiction. It was based on the then-popular theory that the poles of the Earth were holes leading to the interior where an unknown people dwelt. Poe's work was influenced by the writings of the American explorer Jeremiah N. Reynolds, whose "Address on the Subject of a Surveying and Exploring Expedition to the Pacific Ocean and South Seas" Poe reviewed in the same issue of the *Messenger*. Strangely enough, it is thought that this is the Reynolds for whom Poe was said to have called on his deathbed.

Poe was fascinated by the exotic, both fanciful and real. He was rooted in the practical, too, and both exotic and practical called to him from one city. So, the Poes—and Mrs. Clemm—were off to New York.

HARDER TIMES (1837–1843)

"The monthlies of Gotham—Their distinguished Editors, and their vigorous Collaborateurs!" His glass held high, Edgar Allan Poe proposed this toast at the Booksellers Dinner sponsored by the publishers of New York City in March of 1837. It was an event of importance, and Poe was a literary figure of importance, albeit an impoverished one.

The Poes and Mrs. Clemm were living in Greenwich Village in New York City. It was a bad time to be in New York. Financial conditions were rapidly going downhill, and in May the banks suspended specie payments. (Each state had its own currency at that time, and a state's paper notes and bank checks were backed by specie, or a tangible item of value, usually gold.) When people could not redeem their paper money for specie, they felt that their money was worthless and they panicked. The Panic of 1837 in New York City started one of the country's worst depressions, as financial institutions collapsed and brought other businesses down with them.

Poe had been offered a job on the new *New York Review* when he had arrived in the city, but the job seems to have evaporated in the Panic, although one of his reviews was published in the October issue. Poe may have decided not to take the job because he was too busy readying his only novel for publication by Harper & Brothers in New York and Wiley & Putnam in Great Britain. The title is impressive:

*THE NARRATIVE OF
ARTHUR GORDON PYM
OF NANTUCKET.
COMPRISING THE DETAILS OF A MUTINY
AND ATROCIOUS BUTCHERY ON BOARD
THE AMERICAN BRIG GRAMPUS, ON HER
WAY TO THE SOUTH SEAS, IN THE
MONTH OF JUNE, 1827. WITH AN AC-
COUNT OF THE RECAPTURE OF THE
VESSEL BY THE SURVIVERS, THEIR SHIP-
WRECK AND SUBSEQUENT HORRIBLE
SUFFERINGS FROM FAMINE, THEIR DE-
LIVERANCE BY MEANS OF THE BRITISH
SCHOONER JANE GUY; THE BRIEF
CRUISE OF THIS LATTER VESSEL IN THE
ANTARCTIC OCEAN, HER CAPTURE,
AND THE MASSACRE OF HER CREW
AMONG A GROUP OF ISLANDS IN THE
EIGHTY-FOURTH PARALLEL OF SOUTH-
ERN LATITUDE, TOGETHER WITH THE
INCREDIBLE ADVENTURES AND DISCOV-
ERIES STILL FARTHER SOUTH TO WHICH
THAT DISTRESSING CALAMITY GAVE
RISE.*

The preface was signed "A. G. Pym," and acknowl-edgment was given to the assistance of "Mr. Poe, lately editor of the Southern Literary Messenger in preparing this authentic narrative." A "Note" at the end of the text informed readers of "the late sudden and distressing death of Mr. Pym" and stated that this fact had been widely reported by the press. The "Note" continued: "It is feared that the few remaining chapters which were to have completed his narrative . . . have been irrecoverably lost through the accident by which he perished himself."

It was, of course, a hoax, and it was made credible by the note, the preface, and the title page. Readers automatically associated long, detailed titles with nonfiction and simply did not understand that they were being handed a work of fiction. Particularly in England, Poe's hoax was a great success, and people regarded it as truth for many years. Unfortunately, Poe didn't earn any money from his British publisher because the United States was not a participant in the international copyright convention, and the book did not sell well in its American edition.

Other than *Pym* and a critique for the October issue of the *New York Review,* only two works by Poe appeared in 1837, both of them minor. Compared to Poe's prolific output in previous years, this was negligible, indeed. This small output could not be blamed on drink, an issue increasingly raised about Poe. A reputable New York bookseller, William Gowing, who boarded with the Poes and Mrs. Clemm for eight months, stated in later years that he never in that time saw Poe drunk or ungentlemanly, and he saw him every day.

Sometime in early 1838, Poe finally gave up on New York, and the family moved to Philadelphia in hopes of improving their lot. Instead, their situation worsened. Friends—James Pedder, a writer, and his daughters, Anne and Bessie—often had to give them help. They were "suffering for want of food . . . and forced to live on bread and molasses for weeks together,"[1] Pedder was to say in an interview fourteen years later.

When Thomas Wyatt offered Poe fifty dollars to help him abridge his *Manual of Conchology* into an inexpensive text format, the money was eagerly accepted. Poe's name appeared in the first edition as author, but it was removed for the second and third editions. Poe also assisted Wyatt with his *Synopsis of Natural History,* but mercifully his name did not appear as author. For Poe was to suffer much condemnation as a "plagiarizer" of the conchology book, which many did not recognize as an authorized abridgement. Every writer Poe had ever castigated for plagiarism while he was a reviewer for *The Southern Literary Messenger*—and there were a number, for Poe liked to pontificate on the subject—now had a chance for revenge. Poe protested that "textbooks are necessarily done in this fashion" (they are), but he was never able to rid himself of the charge of plagiarizing.

Fortunately, Poe soon found steady work. The publisher of *Gentleman's Magazine,* William E. Burton, an actor well known for his comic roles, was having problems: expenditures were high and circulation was not that large. He was willing to let Poe change all that for ten dollars a week. Poe need work only two hours a day and could use the rest of the time to write, provided he wrote for *Gentleman's Magazine.*

Poe's introduction to the magazine was not promising. Burton refused to publish a critical review he had written. He was to reject a number of such reviews in the year Poe worked for him. But Burton wasn't always at the magazine, since his theater engagements took precedence. Thanks to summer stock, the summer issues of the magazine, now called *Burton's (The Gentleman's Magazine)*, contained Poe's meaningful critiques rather than Burton's puffery. And when Burton wasn't looking, Poe started his long-standing attacks on that icon of the day, Henry Wadsworth Longfellow, and the New England literati (as opposed to the New York and southern literati), in what came to be called "the Longfellow Wars."

Poe's "The Fall of the House of Usher" greeted readers of the September 1839 issue of *Burton's*. The reviews were mixed. Most negative comments were aimed at the horror and the supernatural in the stories, seen as representative of the outmoded German school of literature. Poe denied any connection to any particular school or group of writers; he saw his material as uniquely his, which it was.

In December of 1839, the publishers Lea & Blanchard issued a collection of twenty-five of Poe's stories, including "The Fall of the House of Usher," in book form. The book, *Tales of the Grotesque and Arabesque*, had a printing of 750 copies and was undertaken entirely at the publisher's expense. Poe received only a limited number of free copies and the copyright. The book was also given mixed reviews from "slipshod," to "wild, unmeaning, pointless, aimless . . . caricature run mad" to "The author . . . has placed himself in the foremost rank of American writers." Indeed he had. But that didn't put food on the table. And when, in dire financial straits, Poe offered to sell the copyright to the publishers for a few dollars, they laughed at him. Since they had not sold the edition they had printed, what would they do with the copyright? And when Poe offered them eight more tales for a second edition, Lea & Blanchard rejected the stories out of hand.

Poe became a regular contributor to *Alexander's Weekly Messenger* of Philadelphia in 1840. This did not break Burton's commandment, since the *Weekly Messenger* was owned by the man from whom Burton had bought *The Gentleman's Magazine*. At the same time, Poe, who was not content with all this editing, reviewing, and writing, opened a new avenue for his talents: cryptograms. Poe offered to solve any cryptogram or coded message that readers submitted, innovating a puzzle feature in his magazine familiar to us in today's newspapers and magazines. The response was phenomenal; circulation boomed and Poe was inundated with challenges. He solved them all, despite the extreme difficulty of many. Poe's instincts for raising circulation would have made him the most sought-after advertising executive today. Unfortunately, Poe was ahead of his day, and he finally had to stop the feature. It had become so time consuming that it kept him from earning, as he estimated it, "thousands" of dollars from articles and reviews.

Although Poe's reviews were tough, his opinion was valued and sought after. Some thought to gain Poe's favors through kindnesses to Virginia. To a man in Petersburg, Virginia, who offered his wife a pet fawn, Poe wrote, "Mrs. Poe desires me to thank you with all her heart—but, unhappily, I cannot point out a mode of conveyance. What can be done? Perhaps some opportunity may offer itself hereafter—some friend from Petersburg may be about to pay us a visit. In the meantime accept our best acknowledgments, precisely as if the little fellow were already nibbling the grass before our windows in Philadelphia."[2] He also offered to do all he could for the magazine the man was proposing to publish. Poe's reviews may have been acerbic, but his thank-you notes were charming.

Poe now became fast friends with the writer and lawyer, Frederick William Thomas, a former friend of his brother Henry. Through Thomas, Poe also met Jesse Erskine Dow. Dow was an ex-Navy man, a writer, and later an editor of several Washington, D.C., newspapers. Thomas was a delegate to the Whig National Convention, working for the nomination of William Henry Harrison for the presidency. A rally at which the three friends were present turned into a brawl as supporters of the incumbent President Van Buren pelted the Harrison people with bricks.

Heated conventions such as this one often ended in cooling drinks, and a lot has been said about Poe being drunk periodically at this time. Much of the criticism came from a former friend turned implacable enemy, Dr. Thomas Dunn English. English, a physician and poet, described Poe's home life at this time: "I became a frequent visitor to his family. Mrs. Poe was a delicate gentlewoman, with an air of refinement and good breeding, and Mrs. Clemm had more of the mother than the mother-in-law about her. It was some time before I discovered anything about Poe's habits that was not proper." English tells of helping Poe up from the gutter where he found him drunk one night and bringing him home. Mrs. Clemm is supposed to have cried, "You make my Eddy drunk and then you bring him home." Since Mrs. Clemm insisted that her Eddy was never drunk, but ill, this statement by English does not ring true, but must be considered.

Mr. Burton was also spreading the word that any difficulties with his magazine were Poe's fault because he was drunk all the time. In actuality, Burton was milking the magazine for the money to build a new theater in Philadelphia. Burton's pettiness and English's animosity toward Poe have made it virtually impossible to sift truth from exaggeration about Poe's behavior at this time.

By May of 1840, Burton wanted to sell his magazine. The owner, he said, could expect an income of $3,000 to $4,000 a year. This was no mean sum of money in the mid-1800s, and without Poe, the great circulation booster, Burton's magazine could not have offered such profits to a potential buyer. Yet he docked Poe's meager $50 a month salary by $3 a week until Poe repaid the $100 Burton said was owed him. Poe, who always kept meticulously careful records of his debts (even if he was not always able to repay them), insisted that he only owed Burton sixty dollars, and, understandably, was bitter. He was also angry with Burton for having advertised a writing contest for which he seemingly was not planning to award the prize money. There were many submissions, but Burton kept announcing that the number of articles was not sufficient to make a fair judgment. In this way, he could publish articles without paying for them and at the same time boost his circulation with readers avid to follow the contest.

When Poe heard indirectly that the magazine was for sale, making his position there uncertain, he decided to start his own publication, the *Penn Magazine*. Burton found out about this and fired Poe on the grounds that an announcement that Poe would be operating a rival publication would greatly reduce the price he, Burton, could get for *The Gentlemen's Magazine*. Burton did not attempt to reconcile this claim with the one that he spread about Poe being continually drunk; it is hard to explain how Poe could be both the magazine's mainstay and its agent of destruction at the same time. What Burton really feared was that Poe would take the magazine's subscription list and lure customers away, and he wanted him out of the office. Poe, on his part, was relieved to go.

Poe spent the rest of the year soliciting promises of support, subscriptions, and writers for his magazine. His efforts were halted by illness in early December 1840, and publication was postponed from January until March of 1841. In February, however, the Philadelphia banks suspended specie payments for notes in denominations higher than five dollars. A domino effect followed throughout the southern states, where Poe was particularly popular, and his anticipated subscribers evaporated. *The Penn* was postponed indefinitely.

How the Poe family lived during this period is not known. Presumably they had some money laid away, or perhaps the subscriptions to his magazine were not returned, since Poe intended to start it one day in the not-too-distant future. (The great financier Nicholas Biddle, for instance, had taken a four-year subscription in advance for $60, and Poe might have felt justified in not returning the millionaire's money, at least not immediately.) Virginia had also inherited a little money from her Grandmother Poe's estate, which had been finally settled.

At the end of February 1841, the man who bought *Burton's Gentleman's Magazine*, George R. Graham, announced that Poe would be working for him on the newly named *The Casket & The Gentleman's United*. The terrible title was an accurate, if unimaginative, description of Graham's amalgamation of two of his magazines. What would it have been had he included his third magazine, *The Saturday Evening Post*? Graham tried again: *Graham's Ladys' and Gentleman's Magazine*. Was it meant to be plural "Ladys' "? "Gentleman" is singular, so was the apostrophe in "Ladys' " in the wrong place? Graham obviously needed a good editor! He knew he was getting one in Poe. He announced, "It is with pleasure the Proprietor announces, that he has made arrangements with EDGAR A. POE, Esq., commencing with the present number, by which he secures his valuable pen, as one of the editors of the Magazine. MR. POE is too well known in the literary world to require a word of commendation. As a critic he is surpassed by no man in the country; and as in this Magazine his critical abilities shall have full scope, the rod will be very generously, and at the same time, justly administered."[3]

The new editor did *Graham's* proud: his first contribution to the April 1841 edition was "Murders in the Rue Morgue" from what Poe called his "tales of ratiocination," or deduction. Poe had given the world a new art form, the detective story. His detective, Inspector Auguste Dupin, was the progenitor of Sherlock Holmes, Hercules Poirot, Charlie Chan, Perry Mason, Columbo, Jessica Fletcher, and all those other detectives who use their powers of deduction to solve crimes. (Today, the Mystery Writers of America, in their ongoing tribute to the man who started it all, offer an "Edgar" as an award for the best detective story of the year.)

Poe's readers were not aware of this momentous beginning, although "Murders in the Rue Morgue" excited favorable attention and helped Poe double the magazine's circulation by year's end. Even so, it took him a long while to get "The Mystery of Marie Rogêt—a Sequel to the Murders in the Rue Morgue" published so he could earn some extra money. Using the true story of the sensational New York murder of a young woman, Mary Cecilia Rogers, for inspiration, Poe explained his own story to the publisher of the *Boston Nation.*

> *I have . . . handled my design in a manner alto-*
> *gether novel in literature. I have imagined a series of*
> *nearly exact* coincidences *occurring in Paris. A*
> *young grisette [working girl], one Marie Rogêt, has*
> *been murdered under precisely similar circumstances*
> *with Mary Rogers. Thus, under pretence of showing*
> *how Dupin unravelled the mystery of Marie's assas-*
> *sination, I, in reality, enter into a very long and*
> *rigorous analysis of the New York tragedy. No point*
> *is omitted. I examine, each by each, the opinions and*
> *arguments of the press upon the subject, and show*
> *that this subject has been, hitherto,* unapproached.
> *In fact, I believe not only that I have demonstrated*
> *the fallacy of the general idea—that the girl was the*
> *victim of a gang of ruffians—but have* indicated the
> assassin *in a manner which will give renewed impe-*
> *tus to the investigation.* [4]

The police took some time in arriving at Poe's solution to the mystery, which thoroughly disconcerted him. He could not see how any other solution was possible, and indeed there wasn't. But Poe's story went begging, as did "The Pit and the Pendulum," also written at this time.

It is difficult to understand why Poe had problems

placing his stories and why he had to prove himself again and again. At the same time, a plebeian feature he called "Autography"—brief biographies of writers with facsimile signatures appended—was in great demand: By the end of 1841, the circulation of *Graham's* had reached 17,000 readers; three months later, in mid-March of 1842, it had reached 50,000.

While the gigantic increase in profits properly belonged to Graham, he certainly could have done more for the man largely responsible for earning those profits for him. Instead, Graham decided the magazine's illustrations were responsible for the increase in circulation and began to improve on their quality. To Poe's disgust, Graham was soon paying more for an engraving for a single issue than he paid Poe in salary for two years! The cost of the engravings probably offset most of the gains the magazine had achieved in circulation, and since steel engravings could not be used beyond 50,000 copies without wearing out, *Graham's* booming circulation was ultimately undermined by the additional costs.

Poe wasn't against illustrations, but he insisted that they be pertinent, not gaudy exercises in decoration or fashion plates that were not connected to the text. He began dreaming of his own magazine again, one in which he would do everything right. Graham had discussed the possibility of backing Poe after *Graham's* was solidly established, but he was showing no inclination to keep his word now that the time had come.

Dreams sometimes take a long while to come true, and Poe's friend, Frederick William Thomas, suggested that meanwhile Poe might apply for a good steady job with the government in Washington. Thomas had ob-

tained such a sinecure with "Uncle Sam, who, however slack he may be to his general creditors, pays his
officials with due punctuality. How would you like it:
You stroll to your office a little after nine in the morning leisurely, and you stroll from it a little after two in
the afternoon homeward to dinner, and return no
more that day. If during office hours you have anything
to do it is an agreeable relaxation from the monstrous
laziness of the day. You have on your desk everything
in the writing line in apple-pie order, and if you choose
to lucubrate in a literary way, why you can lucubrate."[5]
Poe's response was, of course, affirmative and immediate. He contacted everyone he knew who could help
him gain such employment, but he soon found out
that getting government work was going to take time.
Meanwhile his need for money was more desperate
than ever.

Early in 1842, as Virginia was singing for a group
of their friends one evening, she suffered a hemorrhage—the sign of advanced tuberculosis. Poe and
Mrs. Clemm insisted that it was an accident, that the
strain of singing had ruptured a blood vessel in Virginia's throat, and they would never accept the omi-
nous diagnosis. A Poe neighbor reminisced about this
event in later years:

> She could not bear the slightest exposure, and needed
> the utmost care; and all those conveniences as to
> apartment and surroundings which are so important
> in the care of an invalid were almost [a] matter of life
> and death to her. And yet the room where she lay for
> weeks, hardly able to breathe except as she was
> fanned, was a little place with the ceiling so low over
> the narrow bed that her head almost touched it. But

Elizabeth Arnold Poe.
This miniature was given
to her son Edgar
on her deathbed.

The young Edgar Allan Poe
was something of a dandy
when he was at the
University of Virginia.
He was said to have
ordered seventeen waistcoats
at one time, then left
the bill to the infuriated
John Allan to pay.

Poe's room at the University of Virginia, now a memorial

John Allan, Poe's foster father

Frances Keeling Allan,
Poe's foster mother

*Poe's own sketch
of his young sweetheart,
Elmira Royster*

*Elmira Royster Shelton
in later years*

John Pendleton Kennedy,
author, senator, and
Poe's early mentor

Thomas Willis White,
who gave Poe his
first publishing job

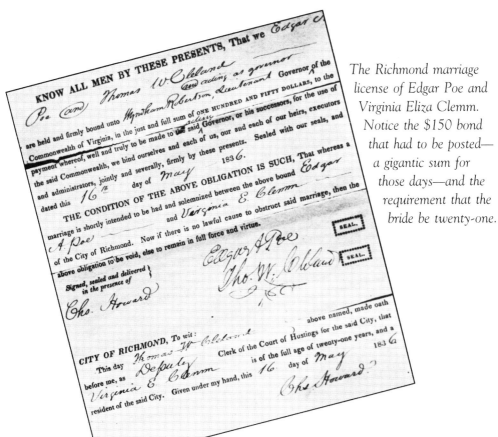

The Richmond marriage license of Edgar Poe and Virginia Eliza Clemm. Notice the $150 bond that had to be posted—a gigantic sum for those days—and the requirement that the bride be twenty-one.

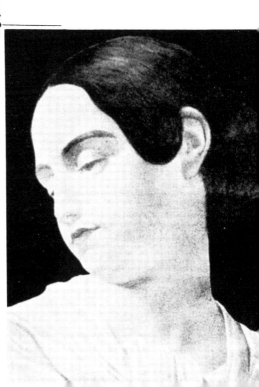

The only known likeness of Virginia Clemm Poe, said to be sketched on her deathbed, when it was suddenly realized that there were no pictures of Poe's young wife

Maria Poe Clemm,
Edgar's aunt,
mother-in-law,
and beloved "Muddy,"
in her widow's cap

Frances Sargent Osgood.
This is an engraving
by John Sartain of a
portrait painted by her
husband, Samuel Osgood.

Sarah Anna Lewis,
whom Poe professed to
dislike, but who assisted
him after Virginia's death
and sheltered Mrs. Clemm
for some time after
Poe's death

Poe's enemies:
(Left) Rufus W. Griswold
(Bottom, left)
Thomas Dunn English
(Bottom, right)
Elizabeth Ellet

A Valentine.

By Edgar A. Poe.

To ___ ___ ___

For her this rhyme is penned, whose luminous eyes,
  Brightly expressive as the twins of Leda,
Shall find her own sweet name that, nestling, lies
  Upon the page, enwrapped from every reader.
Search narrowly these lines! — they hold a treasure
  Divine — a talisman — an amulet
That must be worn at heart. Search well the measure —
  The words — the syllables! Do not forget
The trivialest point, or you may lose your labor!
  And yet there is in this no Gordian knot
Which one might not undo without a sabre
  If one could merely comprehend the plot.
Enwritten upon the leaf where now are peering
  Eyes scintillating soul, there lie perdus
Three eloquent words oft uttered in the hearing
  Of poets, by poets — as the name is a poet's, too.
Its letters, although naturally lying
  (Like the knight Pinto — Mendez Ferdinando —)
Still form a synonym for Truth. — Cease trying!
You will not read the riddle though you do the best you can do.

Valentine's Eve, 1848.

Manuscript copies of two of Poe's poems.
"A Valentine" is the famous—and
difficult—acrostic of Frances Sargent
Osgood's name and also shows how Poe
pieced his manuscript papers together
in long strips for rolling.

To ———.

I heed not that my earthly lot
    Hath — little of Earth in it —
That years of love have been forgot
    In the hatred of a minute : —
I mourn not that the desolate
    Are happier, sweet, than I,
But that you sorrow for my fate
Who am a passer by.

E. A. P

A daguerreotype of Poe reproduced with his autograph

The Poe cottage at Fordham as it looks today.
Once a country retreat, it is now a memorial
in the middle of a bustling metropolis.
(Note city bus going by in background.)

*Sarah Helen Whitman,
Poe's "Helen of a
Thousand Dreams"
and almost his wife*

*Poe's great love,
Annie Richmond*

An engraving of the daguerreotype of Poe
taken by the famous photographer, Matthew Brady

The title page of John Sartain's magazine
and the rather angry foreword to the "first"
appearance of Poe's supposedly last poem,
his great "Annabel Lee"

POE'S LAST POEM.

In the December number of our Magazine we announced that we had another poem of Mr. Poe's in hand, which we would publish in January. We supposed it to be his last, as we received it from him a short time before his decease. The sheet containing our announcement was scarcely dry from the press, before we saw the poem, *which we had bought and paid for*, going the rounds of the newspaper press, into which it had found its way through some agency that will perhaps be hereafter explained. It appeared first, we believe, in the New York Tribune. If we are not misinformed, two other Magazines are in the same predicament as ourselves. As the poem is one highly characteristic of the gifted and lamented author, and more particularly, as our copy of it differs in several places from that which has been already published, we have concluded to give it as already announced.

ANNABEL LEE.

A BALLAD.

BY EDGAR A. POE.

It was many and many a year ago,
   In a kingdom by the sea,
That a maiden there lived whom you may know
   By the name of Annabel Lee;
And this maiden she lived with no other thought
   Than to love and be loved by me.

The poet's grave site. Virginia Poe and Mrs. Clemm are also buried here and memorialized on the sides of the monument.

*no one dared to speak—Mr. Poe was so sensitive
and irritable; "quick as steel and flint," said one
who knew him in those days. And he would not
allow a word about the danger of her dying—the
mention of it drove him wild.*[6]

Virginia recovered from this initial attack, but she was
to hemorrhage again in early June, and again and
again, each time dashing Poe's hopes for her recovery.
Although these attacks went on for five years, the
family continued to insist that bronchitis was the
cause. Poe was later to say that this "horrible never-
ending oscillation between hope & despair" had made
him seek what comfort he could find in alcohol.

Poe asked Graham for an advance of two month's
salary on the day after Virginia's almost fatal hemorrhage, when he needed money for special care for her.
He wrote to Thomas that although he was "entirely
out of (Graham's) debt . . . he not only flatly but
discourteously refused. Now that man *knows* that I
have rendered him the most important services. . . .
If instead of a paltry salary, Graham had given me a
tenth of his Magazine, I should feel myself a rich man
to-day."[7]

Poe pushed himself to continue writing when Virginia became ill, and he did well despite his torment.
An article he did on Henry Wadsworth Longfellow in
the early days of Virginia's illness was lauded as "the
most masterly critique . . . from an American pen."
And another writer said, "His recent review of *Barn-
aby Rudge* [by Charles Dickens] is a masterpiece of
ingenuity." Poe met with Dickens in March while the
great English author was on a tour of the United
States. They had two long discussions about poetry,

and Dickens agreed that, should he decide to write for any American magazine, it would be for *Graham's*. It was a substantial coup for Poe as the magazine's editor.

But the handwriting was on the wall for Poe. Just a few weeks previously, Graham had hired three more editors, two of them women. The *Baltimore Saturday Visiter* had commented, "Graham announces too many editors—if they be *really* editors?. . . So many cooks will spoil his broth for him. In the way of the critical dishes, we want no French or fashionable cooks. Poe is sufficient. He may give homely fare, but it will be honestly served. We are glad to find that, owning to the aforenamed arrangement, or some other cause, Mr. Poe has given real *reviews* this month. All the better. Give him room. He will do much good. We want just such fearless fellows."[8] They were not to get Poe, however, at least not in *Graham's*. On April 1, Poe resigned.

Poe wrote to his friend Thomas,

> *The report of my having parted company with Graham, is correct; although, in the forthcoming June number, there is no announcement to that effect. . . . My duties ceased with the May number. I shall continue to contribute occasionally. Griswold succeeds me. My reason for resigning was disgust with the namby-pamby character of the Magazine—a character which it was impossible to eradicate—I allude to the contemptible pictures, fashion-plates, music and love tales. The salary, moreover, did not pay me for the labor which I was forced to bestow. With Graham who is really a very gentlemanly, although an exceedingly weak man, I had no misunderstanding.*[9]

The usual story of Poe's leave-taking is that he walked into his office one day after a bout of drinking and found Rufus Griswold working at his (Poe's) desk, so he turned and walked out. This is another of the many fables published about Poe, which was fostered by Graham's failure to publish a notice of Poe's resignation in the June issue of his magazine. Had he done so, there would have been no ambiguity about the dates when Poe left and Griswold took over. Instead, a number of inferior writings were laid at Poe's doorstep instead of at Griswold's by those who assumed Poe was still editor of *Graham's.*

Rufus Griswold's place in Poe biography from this time on is ambiguous, not to say mysterious. Poe had met Griswold briefly in the spring of 1841, when he hoped to be mentioned in the anthology Griswold was preparing, *The Poets and Poetry of America.* Poe's poetry at that time was still less known than his critical writings and tales. In fact, when the volume did appear, *The Poet's Magazine* mentioned in its review,

> . . . *who ever thought before Mr. Griswold informed them of the fact, that Edgar A. Poe was entitled to a place among the Poets of America? Who ever dreamed that the cynical critic, the hunter up of small things, journeyman editor of periodicals, and Apollo's man of all work, was a favourite of the Muses, or wrote* Poetry? *It is certainly a "grotesque" discovery* [a play on words from Poe's Tales of the Grotesque and Arabesque] *and, we conjecture, had not Mr. P. taken particular pains to impress the fact upon Mr. Griswold's mind, the world would have remained in happy ignorance of his poetical abilities.* [10]

Poe was not so grateful to Griswold as to puff his review of *The Poets and Poetry of America* to the extent Griswold anticipated. Instead, Poe repeatedly pointed out the book's shortcomings and incurred Griswold's undying enmity, only thinly veiled by a facade of friendship that broke frequently over the years. As the new editor of *Graham's Magazine*, Griswold was accused by an anonymous writer to a Washington paper "of . . . malignant, unjust, and disgraceful attacks on the literary character of its former editor, Mr. Poe." Could Mr. Poe have been the anonymous writer?

By the end of June 1842, Poe was in New York looking for a job and trying to find a publisher for a book of his tales. He also intended to look up his early sweetheart, Mary Starr, now married to a merchant tailor named Jenning. Mary had visited the Poes briefly in Philadelphia, and Poe was to return the visit. He went to Mr. Jenning's business establishment, got his home address in Jersey City, and took off on a ferry from Manhattan. Apparently, he forgot the address and went back and forth on the ferry for several trips until he either remembered it or found someone who knew the Jennings (which is how the story is told by biographers who seem to have thought that Jersey City at that time was little more than a tiny hamlet where everyone knew one another).

Mary Starr Jenning, who is known for somewhat exaggerating her role in Poe's life, told this version over forty years later. She spoke of Poe as being drunk, although why Mr. Jenning would give his wife's address to a drunken Poe was never explained.

> Poe staid to tea with us, but ate nothing; only drank a cup of tea. . . . He then went away (supposedly

after shouting at Mary that she loved him, not her husband.) A few days afterward Mrs. Clemm came to see me, much worried about "Eddie dear," as she always addressed him. She did not know where he was, and his wife was almost crazy with anxiety. I told Mrs. Clemm that he had been to see me. A search was made, and he was finally found in the woods on the outskirts of Jersey City, wandering about like a crazy man. Mrs. Clemm took him back with her to Philadelphia.[11]

Poe could not have been wandering about the woods drunk for these several days—he would have had no access to alcohol. Nor could he have managed without food for that length of time and still been able to wander, although he could have come across enough water to keep him alive. The time frame may have been less than "a few days." Or he may have been suffering from an attack of that same mysterious disease that we know nothing about. Or, of course, there may not have been any wandering in the woods at all, and this might be another fable adding to the mystery of Edgar Allan Poe.

We do know that about this time, Poe was in Philadelphia, where, on the 29th of June, he received a letter from an admirer, James Herron, with a gift of twenty dollars. Herron, a Washingtonian, wrote that he had spoken to Robert Tyler, son of the president (John Tyler had succeeded Harrison, who had died shortly after his inauguration in 1841), about a government appointment for Poe. Poe's friends, Thomas and Dow, were also working on getting him a government position, and he was sure that between them all, they would be successful.

A new customs house inspector in Philadelphia was hiring people, and Poe was promised a place. The promise was never kept, though, and the man treated Poe rudely, to boot. No job, no money—Poe's plans for *The Penn* came to a standstill. But not for long. By January 1843, Poe revived his plans for his own magazine, now renamed *The Stylus* so that it would not seem too local a publication. More sensibly this time, Poe took on a partner, Thomas C. Clarke, publisher of *The Saturday Museum*, who was to finance the venture. They signed on an illustrator, Felix Darley, to provide illustrations at $7 each, "only in obvious illustration of the text and in strict keeping with the Magazine character."[12] Poe insisted on this and other aspects of artistic control over the magazine, one he envisioned as of the highest quality in content, printing, and paper. Sadly, however, Clarke soon found himself in financial difficulties, and in May, he withdrew from the partnership.

Finances may not have been the only reason for Clarke's withdrawal. He was worried about Poe's character. When the renewed possibility of a customs house appointment arose for Poe under another inspector, Poe had hastened to Washington to meet with Robert Tyler about it, hoping also to meet the president himself. Clarke had loaned him the money for the trip, but Poe had to stay longer than anticipated because of the illness of his friend Thomas, who was to take him to the White House. During the days of waiting, Poe had occasion to drink wine with old friends. He had turned snappish, and even the ever-patient Thomas complained of his petulance.

Poe had also managed to vex the wife of his friend Jesse Dow. Dow had written to Clarke to come for

Poe. Dow was at this time a lobbyist for several interests and understood the Washington climate, which
he was afraid would turn against his friend. Clarke, a
teetotaler, was appalled. He did not go to Poe's rescue,
but Poe made the train trip back to Philadelphia without any assistance. He hastened to see Clarke to reassure him of his sobriety, calling Dow's concern
excessive. The damage had been done, however, and
may well have been a deciding factor in Clarke's decision to withdraw.

The Washington trip could not have been such a
terrible fiasco as Dow pictured—Robert Tyler sent Poe
a written recommendation for him to give to the new
Collector of Customs. John Tyler, another son of the
president, also had a conversation with his father
about Poe's needs. The president had virtually reached
the point of deciding on a presidential appointment
for Poe when they were interrupted by official business, and the matter was never reopened. On top of
this piece of bad luck, *The Spirit of the Times* reported
that ". . . the Custom House is beset with an army of
eager applicants for office, and name after name is
diligently sought after to append to petitions and recommendations. All this indicates the hardness of the
times. Thousands of men are ready and anxious to take
public office now, who, in ordinary times, would rather
trust to their own independent exertions for a living."[13] It was not only Poe's behavior in Washington
that deprived him of the security of a government job,
as many biographers would have it. It was also the
hard times, the quirk of timing, bad luck . . . or any
combination thereof.

SUPERSTAR
(1843–1845)

On the 14th of June, 1843, *The Dollar Newspaper* carried the announcement: ". . . the *first prize* of ONE HUNDRED DOLLARS [is awarded] to 'THE GOLD BUG,' which we find, on examination of the private notes sent us, and which no one of the members of the [Selection] Committee has seen, was written by Edgar A. Poe, Esq., of this city—and a capital story the Committee pronounce it to be."

Felix Darley, whom Poe had chosen to illustrate *The Stylus*, recalled Poe reading "The Gold Bug" to him before it was published, so that he could illustrate it:

> He impressed me as a refined and very gentlemanly man; exceedingly neat in his person; interesting always, from the intellectual character of his mind, which appeared to me to be tinged with sadness. His manner was quiet and reserved; he rarely smiled. . . . The form of his manuscript was peculiar: he wrote on half sheets of note paper, which he pasted together at the ends, making one continuous piece, which he rolled up tightly. As he read he dropped it upon the floor. It was very neatly written, and without corrections. [1]

"The Gold Bug," a story of buried treasure, was an immediate sensation, caused huge numbers of *The Dol-*

lar Newspaper to be sold, and was dramatized for the stage. But that one hundred dollars was all Poe received, and it was soon gone. And if that weren't bad enough, a disgruntled reader claimed that the whole contest was a hoax. Poe instituted a suit for slander against the man, who immediately retracted his statement and made a public apology.

Then Poe was attacked as having plagiarized the story from one written by a young girl several years before. Her story was examined by the editors of many publications; each and every one said that there was no resemblance at all between the stories except that a treasure of money was found at the end. That barely removed the stain from Poe's reputation, and the accusation continued to be levied against him even after his death, always in tandem with the old charges of plagiarizing the conchology textbook.

Poe was surrounded by slander. As far away as Jackson, Tennessee, an old acquaintance, John Tomlin, received a letter full of malicious lies about Poe. Tomlin warned Poe that someone in Philadelphia was maligning him, and Poe responded:

> *I believe I know the villain's name. It is Wilmer. In Philadelphia no one speaks to him. He is avoided by all as a reprobate of the lowest class. Feeling a deep pity for him, I endeavoured to befriend him, and you remember that I rendered myself liable to some censure by writing a review of his filthy pamphlet called the "Quacks of Helicon." He has returned my good offices by slander behind my back. All here are anxious to have him convicted—for there is scarcely a gentleman in Phila. whom he has not libelled, through the gross malignity of his nature. Now, I ask*

you, as a friend and as a man of noble feelings, to
send me his letter to you. [2]

Tomlin did send him the letter, and Poe was able to
confirm that it was indeed from Wilmer. Poe and he
had been very close friends years before, but they saw
one another only occasionally when they were both in
Philadelphia. Why Wilmer suddenly chose to defame
Poe in this fashion is unknown. Wilmer's daughter,
Elizabeth, was to become a staunch defender of Poe
and a foe of Griswold's, lending credence to the theory
that Griswold orchestrated this attack and many others on Poe in order to advance his own reputation by
comparison.

Gossip and rumors about Poe were falling on fertile ground, and after a while they took on their own
life: they didn't need a Wilmer or a Griswold to spread
them. Probably because of Poe's growing fame, they
grew from the slightest fluff. Of course, Poe might
have been drinking more, but he could not have been
as productive as he was if he had been incapacitated by
drunkenness as often as was rumored. He had also
taken to the lecture circuit at this time, the end of
1843, and was speaking before packed audiences in
Philadelphia, Baltimore, Wilmington, and Reading
(Pennsylvania)—not something he could have done if
he were always incapacitated by alcohol and subsequent illness.

In early April 1844, suddenly—or so it seems because there is no documentation of events leading to
the decision—the Poes were off for New York once
again. Poe wrote to Mrs. Clemm, whom they left behind until they could afford to send for her, "We went
in the cars to Amboy about 40 miles from N. York,

and then took the steamboat the rest of the way—Sissy [Virginia] coughed none at all. When we got to the wharf it was raining hard. I left her on board the boat, after putting the trunks in the Ladies' Cabin, and set off to buy an umbrella and look for a boarding house."

He had no problem finding either. The boarding house in particular sounds very sheltering, and Poe described the enormous amounts of food served there. He went on, "We have now got 4 $ and a half left. Tomorrow I am going to try & borrow 5 $—so that I might have a fortnight to go upon. I feel in excellent spirits and haven't drank a drop—so that I hope soon to get out of trouble. The very instant I scrape to-gether enough money I will send it on. You can't imagine how much we both do miss you. Sissy had a hearty cry last night, because you and Catterina [their cat] weren't here."[3]

Poe added a reminder to Mrs. Clemm to return a borrowed volume of an early *Southern Literary Messenger* issue to his friend and attorney, Henry Hirst. But Mrs. Clemm had sold the volume at some point to a bookseller, from whom Hirst had to buy it back. The incident was distorted into one of cheating and theft on Poe's part that was passed down in literary history until sufficient research was done to ascertain the true facts. It might have been an honest mistake on Mrs. Clemm's part, or she might have needed the money to survive: she was not to join the Poes for a month. But it was another calumny heaped upon Poe's head, and he could ill afford it.

Within a week of the Poes' arrival in New York City, Poe sold an article to the New York *Sun* and made as spectacular an entrance onto the New York newspaper scene as anyone could hope for. A special edition—called a stop-press—announced:

ASTOUNDING INTELLIGENCE BY PRIVATE EXPRESS FROM CHARLESTON VIA NORFOLK! — THE ATLANTIC OCEAN CROSSED IN THREE DAYS!! — ARRIVAL AT SULLIVAN'S ISLAND OF A STEERING BALLOON INVENTED BY MR. MONCK MASON!!!

The block around the *Sun* building was besieged by thousands of people looking for more news of the Atlantic crossing by air, and in just three days! Copies of the paper were sold at exorbitant prices as readers vied to get more news of the great event. In all, about 50,000 copies of the paper were sold, a huge amount for that time. Of course, rival papers screamed their ridicule as they disclosed the hoax, but good entertainment was had by all, thanks to Poe's fertile imagination.

The following month, Poe became the New York correspondent of a small weekly newspaper, the Columbia, Pennsylvania, *Spy*. It did not hold him for long, although he continued to contribute occasionally to that paper and to *Graham's* and *The Dollar Newspaper* as well.

By early October 1844, Poe had a steady job. Nathaniel Parker Willis, the editor of the new daily newspaper, *The Evening Mirror*, hired him as a "mechanical paragraphist" at a salary of $15 a week. Willis later wrote,

> It was rather a step downward, after being the chief
> editor of several monthlies, as Poe had been, to come

into the office of a daily journal as a mechanical paragraphist. It was his business to sit at a desk, in a corner of the editorial room, ready to be called upon for any of the miscellaneous work of the moment—announcing news, condensing statements, answering correspondents, noticing amusements—everything but the writing of a "leader," or constructing any article upon which his peculiar idiosyncrasy of mind could be impressed. Yet you remember how absolutely and how good-humoredly ready he was for any suggestion, how punctually and industriously reliable, in the following out of any wish once expressed, how cheerful and present-minded in his work when he might excusably have been so listless and abstracted. We loved the man for the entireness of fidelity with which he served us—himself, or any vanity of his own, so utterly put aside.[4]

It was like having a movie star for a servant.

For Poe was a star, and while he was working for Willis, he became a superstar. In January 1845, *The Evening Mirror* published "The Raven." Public response was immediate and ecstatic. The poem was published all over the country, and soon the world. It also came out in book form, *The Raven and Other Poems,* and Poe actually received royalties for the first time.

Poe's fame was so great that when he went to the theater, the star of the production inserted the Raven's refrain, "Nevermore," into his lines, and the audience applauded Poe. "Nevermore" became a catchword around the country, and wherever Poe went, he was introduced triumphantly as "The Raven!" It was an appropriate nickname for Poe, who almost always dressed in black and had piercing, melancholy dark eyes. People sought his autograph—even cut his signature from notes and letters—and begged for a lock of his hair. He was invited to give lectures and poetry readings, and he became the sought-after guest of the first hostess of a literary salon in the United States, Anne C. Lynch, a New York bluestocking. "Bluestocking" was the name given to women of intellect and education who engaged in literary endeavors. The name came from eighteenth-century England, where such women met informally in groups, wearing simple outfits that invariably included blue wool stockings.

The bluestockings made Poe a social lion. His business affairs also seemed to be looking up. He left *The Evening Mirror* at the end of February 1845 for *The Broadway Journal*, where he was given a contract for one-third of the profits to assist C. F. Briggs as editor and John Bisco as publisher. But Briggs wrote to James Russell Lowell,

> Poe is only an assistant to me, and will in no manner interfere with my own way of doing things . . . and as his name is of some authority I thought it advisable to announce him as an editor. . . . Unfortunately for him (Poe) he has mounted a very ticklish hobby just now, Plagiarism, which he is bent on riding to death, and I think the better way is to let him run down as soon as possible by giving him no check. Wiley & Putnam are going to publish a new edition of his tales and sketches. Every body has been raven mad about his last poem, and his lecture . . . has gained him a dozen or two of waspish foes who will do him more good than harm.[5]

Briggs thought by this last remark that those foes would sting Poe into stopping, but little did he know Poe.

And tragically, despite his part ownership of a magazine and his writing and his star status, Poe wrote to his friend Frederick Thomas in May 1845 that he was "as poor now as ever I was in my life—except in hope, which is by no means bankable."

What with money worries and the numerous social gatherings he was attending, Poe might have relaxed with a glass of port or something stronger now and then. Other people could do this with impunity, but not Poe. Unfortunately, he was recovering from such an evening when, after years of a friendship maintained by correspondence, James Russell Lowell came down from New England to the Poe home to meet him for the first time. Lowell was to write to one of Poe's biographers years later, "I went by appointment & found him a little tipsy, as if he were recovering from a fit of drunkenness, & with that over-solemnity with which men in such cases try to convince you of their sobriety. I well remember (for it pained me) the anxious expression of his wife. . . . The shape of his head was peculiar, broad at the temples, & the forehead sloping backward almost sharply . . . there was something snakelike about it."[6]

Poe didn't think much of Lowell either: "I was very much disappointed in his appearance as an intellectual man. He was not half the noble-looking person that I expected to see."[7] That craze of the day, phrenology, in which character and talents were judged by the shape of the head and its bumps, had apparently influenced both men. Their friendship ended with this first and last look at each other.

Any chance of a reconciliation disappeared when

Poe gave a reading at the Boston Lyceum in October. Invited to present a new poem, instead he read "Al Aaraaf." When the press discovered that he had written the poem years before as a very young man, they raised a great hue and cry over what they considered an impertinence. It gave them great pleasure to take their revenge for Poe's constant attacks on their local favorite, Henry Wadsworth Longfellow. Poe took little notice; he had not been able to write a new poem and felt that there had been so few readers of "Al Aaraaf," it had to be new to most of the audience!

The year 1845 was a busy one for Poe, although most of what he published was not new. There simply wasn't enough time to create new material when he had to fill the pages of a weekly magazine. The magazine was having partner trouble as well. Briggs wanted to buy out Bisco and bring in another, more affluent, publisher. Briggs offered fifty dollars to Bisco, who, understandably, thought that the amount was far too little and refused to sell. Briggs finally stopped trying to get rid of Bisco and surrendered his own share in the magazine instead. Now it was Bisco and Poe. By October, it was just Poe.

Thomas Dunn English had loaned Poe $30 toward buying Bisco out. Horace Greeley, the legendary newspaperman who is best remembered for the advice, "Go west, young man!" (not his words, but he could never convince people of that), also loaned Poe $50 in cash and gave him a promissory note for another $50 payable in sixty days. Poe gave Bisco $50 and agreed to pay him $300 more in three months. It was certainly a much better offer than Briggs had made Bisco, and it was probably too much.

Poe finally had his own magazine. But buying a magazine and keeping it going were two different things, particularly when it was in trouble even before the sale. It was too much for Poe. Despite his calls on those who owed him money, on friends, and even on those who were somewhat less than friends, like Griswold, who might lend him money, and despite his quickly taking on a business partner, the magazine folded less than three months after Poe bought it.

Business affairs were not Poe's only worry. Entangling alliances with women were becoming even more troublesome. There was the incident of the visit to Mary Starr Jenning in 1841, if it was indeed true. Then, in the summer of 1843, Poe had visited Saratoga Springs, in upstate New York. He may have gone there for his health, for it was a noted spa as well as a resort. At Saratoga, Poe had met a Mr. and Mrs. John Barhyte. Mrs. Barhyte was a poet, and she and Poe enjoyed one another's company. Tongue-waggers made much of this, although there was no indication of any relationship between them other than friendship on several summer visits.

But these were minor incidents in light of what was to come.

CHAPTER SIX

A WAY
WITH WOMEN
(1845–1848)

As a boy, Edgar Poe had addressed loving poems to the young girls he knew. As a young man, Poe had indulged in several fleeting romances with young women. As a mature married man, his interest in women did not wane.

Poe's next encounter after Saratoga and Mrs. Barhyte was more extensive and more enigmatic. It took place in 1845 and involved Frances Sargent Osgood, the mother of two.

Was it a flirtation or an affair, an affair that resulted in the birth of Mrs. Osgood's third child, Fanny Fay? We cannot know with certainty. Mrs. Osgood was one of the New York bluestockings, and Poe had reviewed her poetry favorably, as he did for most women poets. (He particularly admired Elizabeth Barrett Barrett [later Barrett Browning], to whom he had dedicated *The Raven and Other Poems*.)

Poe had asked a friend to introduce him to Mrs. Osgood, and she reminisced about their first meeting a few years later,

> *I shall never forget the morning when I was summoned to the drawing-room [of the Astor House] to receive him. With his proud and beautiful head erect,*

*his dark eyes flashing with the elective light of feeling
and of thought, a peculiar, an inimitable blending of
sweetness and hauteur in his expression and manner,
he greeted me, calmly, gravely, almost coldly; yet
with so marked an earnestness that I could not help
being deeply impressed by it. From that moment
until his death we were friends, although we met only
during the first year of our acquaintance. During
that year, while travelling for my health, I maintained a correspondence with Mr. Poe, in accor-
dance with the earnest entreaties of his wife, who
imagined that my influence over him had a restrain-
ing and beneficial effect. It had, as far as this—that
having solemnly promised me to give up the use of
stimulants, he so firmly respected his promise to me,
as never once, during the whole acquaintance, to
appear in my presence when in the slightest degree
affected by them.[1]*

Mrs. Osgood became Virginia Poe's good friend
and visited Virginia often since she was by this time
too ill to travel. Virginia seems to have had no reser-
vations over Mrs. Osgood's relationship with her husband. She knew her husband well, and she knew the
place she had in his heart and life. Poe did enjoy the
company of women, and Virginia, sick and exhausted
much of the time, loved her Eddie enough to encour-
age it. There are those who find it difficult to understand Virginia's feelings and condemn her (some going
so far as to call her "retarded") for being so "uncaring." To the contrary, such a gesture could have only
come from a deeply caring heart.

Poe and Mrs. Osgood met one another frequently
and published a number of romantic poems addressed

to one another quite openly. Their very openness makes it unlikely that they were lovers; people did not flaunt their romantic liaisons in print in those days. Nor was there any damaging gossip about adultery in a day when New York and literary society thrived on gossip. It is also proposed that Samuel Osgood, a famed artist, would not have undertaken to paint Poe's portrait, as he did, if he thought that his wife and Poe were having anything more than an innocent, albeit a flirtatious, relationship. When he painted that portrait is in doubt, however. But he does seem to have been a remarkably complaisant husband. Proponents of the theory of Poe's paternity point to his lovely "Ula-lume—a Ballad," published in December 1847, as a eulogy to Fanny Fay, who died in October of that year. The poem is set ". . . in the lonesome October/ of my most immemorial year," and Poe sometimes said it was his only poem with something autobiographical about it. But it was written the year before Fanny Fay's death at the request of an admirer who felt Poe should address multiple emotions in a single poem and who wanted it for reading aloud. It is very much like music in its sounds and in the wealth of interpretations it has engendered, but only the most determined can see it as a eulogy to Fanny Fay.

Mrs. Osgood had still another gentleman friend, Edward J. Thomas, a merchant. Jealous of Poe, Thomas tried to discredit him with Mrs. Osgood by telling her that Poe was rumored to be a forger. Mrs. Osgood, of course, went to Poe with the rumor, and Poe demanded a retraction from Edward Thomas. The merchant promised to track down the source of the rumor. When he did, he apologized, reporting that the source "denied it *in toto*—says he does *not know it* and never said so—and it undoubtedly arose from the misunderstanding of some word used."[2] Poe was satisfied with this explanation and dropped his plan to sue for defamation of character. Poe's charity in this matter was to be interpreted later as an acknowledgment of the truth of the slander.

A still more unpleasant incident brought the relationship between Poe and Mrs. Osgood to a crashing close. The matter concerned letters and the lies of a truly evil woman. Some of the bluestockings wrote gushing fan letters to Poe that verged on the ridiculous. As was his custom, Poe shared these silly letters with Virginia and Mrs. Clemm. This was not exactly gallant, but the two women particularly enjoyed the laugh they got from them. Some of the letter writers also visited Poe's home on occasion; they hoped to curry favor with Poe by paying attention to his lonely, fading wife. One such woman, Mrs. Elizabeth F. Ellet, walked in on the women as they were having a hearty laugh over one of Mrs. Ellet's notes to Poe, a virtual love letter. Mrs. Ellet was infuriated, and she wanted revenge. She told her bluestocking acquaintances of the incident, but she did not admit that she had sent such a letter. Instead, she said that the letter came from Mrs. Osgood and was exceedingly indiscreet.

Mrs. Osgood, of course, denied any indiscreet letters. She was far too intelligent to engage in this kind of letter writing, particularly since she knew how letters were shared in the Poe household. But two bluestockings took it upon themselves to go to Poe's home and demand all of Mrs. Osgood's letters back. Poe, appalled at their intrusion, and knowing that Mrs. Ellet had stirred up all this ill feeling, suggested that the ladies should tell Mrs. Ellet to be concerned about her own letters, not those of Mrs. Osgood. By the code of the day, this was not a gentlemanly thing for Poe to say, since it implied that the Ellet letters would compromise her reputation.

As soon as the women had left, and without waiting for Mrs. Ellet to ask for her letters, Poe bundled them up and returned them to her home. Mrs. Ellet, trying to appear injured rather than foolish, denied getting the letters back. To improve upon her story, she sent her brother, William Lummis, to defend her honor by demanding the letters back. Lummis threatened to kill Poe if he did not produce the letters, and Poe, of course, could not. Poe borrowed a pistol from Thomas Dunn English to defend himself. English was the wrong man to go to. English and Poe had never really liked one another and had severed their relationship two years before, when a tipsy Poe had poked fun at English. The uneasy truce that had been declared between the men for business purposes now broke. Not only did English refuse to give Poe the pistol, but he accused Poe of lying about having letters from Mrs. Ellet in the first place. Poe flailed out with his fists, English returned the blows, and Thomas Wyatt, who had accompanied Poe, had to break up the fight.

Poe was confined to bed for several days and had his doctor deliver a note of apology to Mrs. Ellet. Its exact contents are a mystery. Poe is said to have told her that he did not recollect making an accusation of indiscretion on her part and could only have done so if he had been suffering from temporary insanity.

The Raven was craven, but an apology was preferable to a duel to the death. Whether or not sudden insanity was actually Poe's excuse, he certainly would

not have had his apology take on the meaning given to
it by Mrs. Ellet. She immediately circulated stories
that Poe was insane and had been placed in various
mental institutions. And when Mrs. Osgood angrily
confronted her once again, Mrs. Ellet, a facile liar,
said that the indiscreet letter must have been a forgery—by Poe. And, she wrote, "Had you seen the fear-
ful paragraphs which Mrs. Poe first repeated and
afterwards pointed out—which haunted me night and
day like a terrifying spectre. . . . It is most unfortunate
both for you & me that we ever had any acquaintance
with such people as the Poes—but I trust the evil is
now at an end."[3]

The evil lay in Mrs. Ellet when she wrote these
lies to Mrs. Osgood. Mrs. Osgood knew it, but she also
knew that Mrs. Ellet would stop at nothing to damage
her reputation if she were to maintain any further
contact with the Poes. So there were no more letters
and no more visits to the lonely Virginia. There were
two or three additional published poems from Mrs.
Osgood to Poe and a mention or two by Poe of her
work. For Valentine's Day, 1846, Poe composed a
complicated acrostic poem of Mrs. Osgood's name.
Then there was nothing more, despite Mrs. Osgood's
claim to having been Poe's friend until death—perhaps she meant in spirit.

That same Valentine's Day, Virginia Poe sent an
acrostic valentine to her beloved husband that shows
her weariness at the ugliness that had invaded their
lives as Poe's fame grew.

Ever with thee I wish to roam—
Dearest my life is thine.
Give me a cottage for my home

And a rich old cypress vine,
Removed from the world with its sin and care
And the tattling of many tongues.
Love alone shall guide us when we are there—
Love shall heal my weakened lungs;
And Oh, the tranquil hours we'll spend,
Never wishing that others may see!
Perfect ease we'll enjoy, without thinking to lend
Ourselves to the world and its glee—
Ever peaceful and blissful we'll be.

A few months later Poe brought Virginia and Mrs.
Clemm to a cottage in the country at Fordham, today
very much a bustling part of New York City, but in
those days farmland connected to the city by only two
trains a day. Neither tranquility, bliss, nor health
found its way to Fordham, however.

The enmity between Poe and Thomas Dunn English became serious. English was a jack-of-all-trades
—a doctor, lawyer, editor, poet—but a master of
none. For the July 1846 issue of *Godey's Lady's Book,*
Poe contributed the first of a series of "Sketches of the
New York Literati," among which there was a humor-
ous, but patronizing, sketch of English as an editor
who did not know English. English's fury was mania-
cal, and his response to Poe was printed in *The Evening
Mirror:* Poe had borrowed money from him under false
pretenses—he had assured English that *The Broadway
Journal* would be a profitable venture and it had not
turned out so; Poe had tacitly admitted that he was a
forger because he had dropped his lawsuit against Edward Thomas; Poe "told me [English] that he had vil-
ified a certain . . . authoress [Mrs. Ellet]. . . ."; Poe
was a drunkard, "thoroughly unprincipled, base and

depraved . . . not alone an assassin in morals, but a quack in literature." English went on and on, and the editors of *The Evening Mirror* enjoyed the chance to publish it all, somehow not understanding or caring that they might be printing libelous material.

Poe sued the *Mirror*, and the New York literati lined up on either side. Back and forth between friend and foe it went, drawing in journals from around the country. It was called "The War of the Literati," and it did wonders for circulation and thus the publishers' income. *Godey's Lady's Book* had to go back to press, and Godey even attempted to buy back copies of the July issue containing the sketch of English so he could resell them. He could not keep up with the demand for later issues, either. But Poe gave up the "Literati" after the fourth installment—people were taking the sketches too seriously, when his design was to present "critical gossip."

Poe also realized from the unexpectedly huge response that a book on the literati might be in order. It was a good time to stay in Fordham, to concentrate on serious writing, and to keep a low profile. The low profile didn't work, either. Every disgruntled figure ever wounded by the prick of Poe's pen saw the chance for vindication by claiming Poe was sick with a brain malady or was a madman in an institution. Godey, thriving on the whole affair, did manage to shake a weak fist at Poe's defamers: "We have the name of one person. . . . Mr. Poe has been ill, but we have letters from him of very recent dates, also a new batch of the Literati, which show anything but feebleness either of body or mind."

The writing should have shown feebleness of body, for the Poes were virtually starving in Fordham.

When Poe was ill, he could not write. When he could not write, he did not get paid. His work made circulation and profits climb, but Poe gained nothing but notoriety. Mrs. Clemm picked up donations of food from the owners of the farm they lived on, or she collected edible greens from the fields. If there was enough money for carfare, she took the train into the city and peddled Poe's poems for reprint. Publishers learned to dread seeing her, with a large basket over her arm, on their doorstep. Her meekness, her patient but persistent begging, her promises of Poe's favors— all made them feel guilty and annoyed at the same time.

There was worse to come. By fall, Poe could not work at all—his beloved Virginia was dying.

Mrs. Clemm contacted Mary Gove, a novelist and health reformer, for help. Her daughter Virginia was "dying of want," she wrote, and Poe was "very ill." Mrs. Gove (who was to become Mary Gove Nichols after a divorce and remarriage) recalled her first visit to the cottage in Fordham:

> The autumn came, and Mrs. Poe sank rapidly in consumption, and I saw her in her bed chamber. Everything here was so neat, so purely clean, so scant and poverty-stricken, that I saw the sufferer with such a heartache as the poor feel for the poor. There was no clothing on the bed, which was only straw, but a snow white spread and sheets. The weather was cold, and the sick lady had the dreadful chills that accompany the hectic fever of consumption. She lay on the straw bed, wrapped in her husband's [West Point] greatcoat, with a large tortoise-shell cat [Cattarina] on her bosom. The wonderful cat seemed conscious of her

great usefulness. The coat and the cat were the suf-
ferer's only means of warmth, except as her husband
held her hands, and her mother her feet. . . . I came
to New York, and enlisted the sympathies and services
of a lady [Marie Louise Shew], whose heart and hand
were ever open to the poor and miserable. A feath-
erbed and abundance of bed-clothing and other com-
forts were the first fruits of my labour of love. . . .
From the day this kind lady first saw the suffering fam-
ily of the poet, she watched over them as a mother
watches over her babe. . . .[4]

The "kind lady" was Mrs. Marie Louise Shew (later, after a divorce, Mrs. Houghton). She was the daughter and wife of physicians, and in the fashion of the day acted as a physician herself. She ran Dr. Shew's clinic for water cures at a place not far from the Poes. Perhaps there were not many patients, for she spent most of her time giving free medical care and doing social work among the poor of New York City. From the time of her first visit to the Poes at Mrs. Gove's request, in November 1846, she spent almost all her time nursing Virginia and often Poe, who was beside himself with anxiety and grief.

Mrs. Gove and Mrs. Shew were not the Poes' only guardian angels. Mrs. Mary E. Hewitt, a blue-stocking who had remained firmly on Poe's side throughout the Ellet fracas, although not well acquainted with Poe, solicited donations to assist the family. She had some trepidation about publicizing Poe's misfortunes, knowing of his pride, but decided it was the only way to get the money they desperately needed. The newspapers picked up the story, some of them gloating over Poe's circumstances, others preaching, and one or two railing at society's neglect of even its greatest artists.

Nathaniel P. Willis wrote an editorial on Poe's unhappy situation in *The Home Journal*, in which he suggested a "Hospital for Disabled Labourers with the Brain. . . . Here is one of the finest scholars, one of the most original men of genius, and one of the most industrious of the literary profession of our country, whose temporary suspension of labour, from bodily illness, drops him immediately to a level with the common objects of public charity. . . . We received yesterday a letter from an *anonymous hand*, expressing high admiration for Mr. Poe's genius, and enclosing a sum of money with a request that we would forward it to him. . . . [We will] forward any other similar tribute of sympathy."[5]

Some of Poe's enemies had a field day with Willis's proposals. *The Evening Mirror* said, ". . . we propose to add to the building, an asylum for those who have been ruined by the diddlers of the quill. We think it quite possible that *this* apartment might be soonest filled, as we cannot now call to mind a single instance of a man of real literary ability suffering from poverty, who has always lived an industrious, honest and honorable life; while of the other class of indigents, we know of numerous melancholy specimens. . . ." Of course there were others "of real literary ability suffering from poverty," and this was uncalled-for malice, but, then, the magazine was still facing Poe's lawsuit for libel.

Poe wrote to Willis to express his thanks for his "kind and manly comments." He was upset that his private affairs had been "thus pitilessly thrust before the public" and wanted to clarify his situation. It was true that Virginia was hopelessly ill and that he had been "long and dangerously ill" and therefore had not been able to earn money, but he denied ever being in unendurable need. "Even in the city of New York I could have no difficulty in naming a hundred persons, to each of whom—when the hour for speaking had arrived—I could and would have applied for aid. . . . [I am recovering] and have a great deal to do; and I have made up my mind not to die till it is done."[6]

A constant stream of visitors bearing comforts visited the Poe household. Among them was Sarah Anna Lewis, a would-be poet, whose husband paid Poe to edit her work and advise her. Mrs. Shew reminisced many years later, when she was Mrs. Houghton: "Mr. Poe was indebted to [Mrs. Lewis], that is, she paid Mrs. Clemm in advance, when they were needy, and poor Poe *had to notice* her writings, and praise them. He expressed to me the *great mortification it was to him,* and I childlike I hated the fat gaudily dressed woman whom I often found sitting in Mrs. Clemm's little kitchen, waiting to see the man of genius, who had rushed out to escape her, to the fields and forest—or to the grounds of the Catholic school in the vicinity. I remember Mrs. C sending me after him in great secrecy one day & I found him sitting on a favorite rock muttering his desire to die, and get rid of *Literary bores.*"[7]

Elizabeth Willis White, to whom Poe was rumored to have been engaged before his marriage to Virginia, also visited the cottage at Fordham. So did another of Poe's former loves, Mary Starr Jenning. Years later, she recalled—perhaps correctly, perhaps not—"The day before Virginia died I found her in the parlor. I said to her, 'Do you feel any better to-day?'

and sat down by the big arm-chair in which she was placed. Mr. Poe sat on the other side of her. I had my hand in hers, and she took it and placed it in Mr. Poe's, saying, 'Mary, be a friend to Eddie, and don't forsake him; he always loved you—didn't you, Eddie?' "[8]

This same day, Poe sent urgently for Mrs. Shew. "My poor Virginia still lives, although failing fast and now suffering much pain. May God grant her life until she sees you and thanks you once again. Her bosom is full to overflowing—like my own—with a boundless— inexpressible gratitude to you. Lest she may never see you more—she bids me say that she sends you her sweetest kiss of love and will die blessing you. But come—oh come to-morrow."[9]

Mrs. Shew came.

"She called me to her bedside, took a picture of her husband from under her pillow, kissed it and gave it to me. . . . She took from her portfolio a worn letter and showed it to her husband, he read it and weeping heavy tears gave it to me to read. It was a letter from *Mr. Allan's wife* after his death. It expressed a desire to see him [Poe], acknowledged that she alone had been the cause of his adopted Father's neglect."[10] (Many deny this as too improbable and feel that Mrs. Shew confused the first wife with the second, but this, too, seems improbable.)

Virginia Poe died on the thirtieth of January, 1847, at the age of twenty-five. Mrs. Shew wrote that she "bought her coffin, her grave clothes, and Edgar's mourning, except the little help Mary Starr gave me." Mrs. Clemm was forever grateful that Mrs. Shew provided "beautiful linen" rather than ordinary cotton for Virginia to wear in death. And the owners of the cottage Poe rented at Fordham provided a place for Virginia in their family plot in the graveyard of the nearby Fordham Dutch Reformed Church.

From the time of Virginia's death, Poe's detractors have tried to say that she died in want. This was not true. Her needs were met by charitable friends. In her last months, Virginia had wanted for nothing.

The pain of Virginia's death was, of course, great. But for Poe it must have been mixed with relief that the hideous ups and downs of her illness, the hoping and the despair, and finally the waiting for the dreaded and inevitable end, were over. On the manuscript of "Eulalie," Poe's one poem celebrating a happy marriage, he wrote the only poem that bibliographers are sure belongs to Virginia:

> *Deep in earth my love is lying*
> *And I must weep alone.*

Poe expressed his deep gratitude to Marie Louise Shew in a poem, "To M.L.S.," for Valentine's Day, just two weeks after Virginia's death. It was couched in such loving terms that she was embarrassed by it. When he told her of writing yet another poem to her, Mrs. Shew bought it from him at the going rate plus five dollars so that it would not be published: "It was so very personal and complimentary, I dreaded the ordeal."

In February, just a few weeks too late for Virginia to rejoice in it, Poe won his lawsuit for libel against *The Evening Mirror.* A jury awarded him $225, plus legal costs, the most money Poe ever had at one time. Mrs. Clemm soon had a silver-plated coffee service to grace her table. But the attacks on Poe, undoubtedly orchestrated by Thomas Dunn English and Mrs. Ellet, took new turns and became still more offensive and coarse. And some of those who had contributed to the fund when Poe was in need suggested he might now return their money.

Whether it was this stress added to that of Virginia's death or something physical, Poe was once again gravely ill, although exactly what his illness was is unknown. Nineteenth-century illnesses were not all the same as those of the twentieth century. Women swooned and fainted and often had an illness called "the vapors," prostration was common among both men and women, and men seemed to suffer a multitude of ills such as "brain congestion," "liver congestion," and "brain fever."

Mrs. Shew took Poe to see a famous physician of the day, Dr. Valentine Mott, at New York University School of Medicine. She wrote of this visit, "I made my Diagnosis and went to the great Dr. Mott with it. I told him that *at best* when he was well Mr. Poe's pulse beat only ten regular beats after which it suspended or intermitted (as Doctors say). I decided that in his best health, he had leasion [lesion] on one side of the brain, and as he could not bear stimulants or tonics, without producing insanity, I did not feel much hope, that he could be raised up from a brain fever, brought on by extreme suffering of mind and body . . . sedatives even had to be administered with caution."[11] Dr. Mott agreed with Mrs. Shew's diagnosis, but what exactly they meant by a "brain leasion" is uncertain.

Mrs. Shew may not have understood the muse that drove the poet, but she understood Poe the patient. She saw that he rested, then she offered him occupational therapy: to furnish and decorate her wealthy bachelor-uncle's new house. Poe's descriptions of furnishings in his writings and the attractiveness of the meager furnishings at Fordham, remarked on by many of the visitors to the home, had clued her into his interests in this area. Poe was delighted with the commission. "Nothing for months, has given me so much real pleasure, as your note of last night [containing her suggestion]. . . . How kind of you to let me do even this small service for you, in return for the great debt I owe you. . . . I know I can please you in the purchases."[12]

It was also the practical Mrs. Shew who helped Poe write one of his more famous poems, "The Bells." In fact, the first draft bears the notation "By Mrs. M. L. Shew." Poe needed a poem and couldn't think of a topic. Distressed, he was discussing his problem with Mrs. Shew at her home in New York City when the bells from nearby churches began their clanging. Mrs. Shew wrote down, " 'The Bells' by E. A. Poe and I mimic[ked] his style, and wrote the Bells, the little silver Bells, &c. &c. he finishing each line."[13] Several others claimed that Poe wrote the poem in their company in other cities, but they might have been part of Poe's reworking of these beginnings into the final version.

Poe was fond of Mrs. Shew, but she was careful to keep him away from the subject of a closer relationship. He hinted at it frequently—Poe wanted romance, and he wanted to be loved, desires not unusual in a recent widow or widower. He said he wanted marriage and he went in pursuit of a wife, but his behavior indicated something different.

Poe decided to visit Elmira Royster Shelton, his sweetheart at sixteen, who was now a widow with two

children and still living in Richmond. There is a dif-
ference of opinion as to whether he met her or not in
the summer of 1847. He said he did, but Mrs. Clemm
insisted Poe was not gone long enough from Fordham
to have reached Richmond. At any rate, Mrs. Shelton
did not reenter his life at this time.

Poe definitely reached Washington, where he visited his old friend, Frederick William Thomas, and
attended a high school graduation at which he was
swamped by admiring young fans. When his money
ran low, he went north to Philadelphia, where he
called on several editors he knew and received an advance from George Graham for an article. But once
again he took ill, and he had to be helped by Robert
T. Conrad, Graham's assistant. Poe later wrote to
thank Conrad for his assistance: "Without your aid, at
the precise moment in which you rendered it, it is
more than probable that I should not now be alive to
write you this letter."[14] Although Poe was given to
occasional embroidering of facts, whatever it was that
was causing his attacks was apparently increasing in
frequency.

Back in New York, Poe thought to look elsewhere than to Mrs. Shelton for a wife. A correspondent from Lowell, Massachusetts, Mrs. Jane Edwina
Locke, had piqued his interest with a poem of sympathy when Virginia was dying. Mrs. Locke's letters were
inclined to be romantic, but Poe was not sure of her
marital status. He was also intrigued by a talented poet
from Providence, Rhode Island, Sarah Helen Whitman, whose work he very much admired. He knew
Mrs. Whitman was a widow, but he was not sure of
what her feelings might be toward him—she was well

known to Mrs. Osgood and to Anne C. Lynch, the bluestocking whose home had been closed to him since Mrs. Ellet had spread her lies about. For the rest of 1847, however, Poe saw only Mrs. Shew and Sarah Anna Lewis (the same Mrs. Lewis he once hid from). Mrs. Lewis spent a good deal of time at Fordham, and Poe reciprocated her kindness to Mrs. Clemm with several reviews of her poetry, using, at Mrs. Clemm's request, some of the puffery he deplored in other reviewers.

Valentine's Day of 1848 saw Poe working on his complex cosmological treatise that he called a "prose poem," *Eureka,* and on his revived plans for his own magazine, *The Stylus.* It also brought Poe a valentine from Sarah Helen Whitman, a poem addressed to him and delivered at the annual valentine reading at the salon of Anne C. Lynch. Poe, flattered, sent Mrs. Whitman a manuscript copy of his poem, "To Helen." He had worked on the poem over the years since it was first inspired by Mrs. Stanard, and it now contained the immortal lines, "The glory that was Greece, and the grandeur that was Rome." In June, Poe sent her a second "To Helen" poem, which opens with a description of how he had once seen her among the roses in her garden in the moonlight. (This occurred during a brief visit to Providence to rendezvous with Mrs. Osgood when they were still on good terms and she was "travelling for her health," possibly to cool down the relationship.)

In late May or early June of 1848, one of Poe's most important mainstays, Mrs. Shew, severed her association with him. He had published what he considered his magnum opus, his treatise on cosmology. It was Poe's pantheistic theory of how the world began and would end—his philosophy of the universe and its life forms as the physical manifestation of God. Mrs. Shew was convinced by a theologian friend that her association with the man who could write such things would affect her spiritual well-being. It is also possible that Poe's emotional intensity and dependency on Mrs. Shew frightened her off—her marriage was in poor shape. (She later got a divorce and married Dr. Houghton in 1850.)

Poe replied to Mrs. Shew's letter of farewell, "Can it be true Louise that you have the idea fixed in your mind to desert your unhappy and unfortunate friend and patient. . . . Oh Louise how many sorrows are before you, your ingenuous and sympathetic nature, will be constantly wounded in contact with the hollow heartless world, and for me alas! unless some true and tender and pure womanly love saves me, I shall hardly last a year longer, alone!"[15] He would last only a little more than a year longer with the love.

THE SEARCH (1848–1849)

" . . . Unless some true and tender and pure womanly love saves me . . ." From what? How? What drove Poe in his frantic search for someone to love him? Was it a sense of impending death? Or was he saying "love" and meaning "support," the financial as well as the emotional support of a woman with money? He could hardly be blamed for looking for security after the years of deprivation he had suffered, yet he would never admit to such an ungallant quest.

Mrs. Edwina Locke was soon eliminated from the list of possible marriage partners. She had arrived in Fordham one day, probably in late June of 1848, and turned out to be married already and the mother of five children. She was not averse to a flirtation, however, and was sure that Poe's tentative exploration of her marital status was tantamount to a declaration of love. To foster the relationship, she convinced Poe to give a lecture in her home city of Lowell, arranged all the details, and put him up at her home.

Now fate stepped in and played a nasty trick—or Poe's frantic search for love overwhelmed his good judgment. Poe decided to pay a call on the Lockes' next-door neighbors and distant relatives, the Richmonds. He rang their bell, Mrs. Richmond opened the door, and Poe fell in love. After giving the lecture Mrs. Locke had arranged, Poe went to the Richmond home to spend the night and the next day. This infuriated Mrs. Locke, who had wanted to show off her celebrity guest. But rather than vent her anger at Poe, she blamed the Richmonds. Poe escaped the ensuing gossip by returning to New York.

Despite his love for Nancy Richmond—whom he called "Annie"—Poe had not forgotten he needed a wife. He turned to Sarah Helen Whitman. For some time, the widowed Providence poet had been making inquiries among friends about Poe, whose sullied reputation made her wary. But when Poe had sent her his poem, "To Helen," she had responded with a poem of her own, sending him two stanzas anonymously. The poem was published in its entirety in *The Home Journal* at the end of July. A mixup in the mail prevented the stanzas from reaching Poe until well after the poem's publication, and when he finally did get them, he was determined to go to Providence to meet Mrs. Whitman at once. He solicited a letter of introduction from a mutual friend, who wrote, "This letter will be handed to you by Mr. Edgar A. Poe. He is already so well known to you that any thing more than the announcement of his name would be an impertinence from me. I feel much obliged to Mr. Poe for permitting me thus to associate myself with an incident so agreeable to both of you, as I feel persuaded your first meeting will prove."[1] That first visit took place on the 21st of September and was very agreeable.

The following evening, Mrs. Whitman had a gathering of friends at her home to meet Poe. The reminiscence of one of those friends is thought to refer to this evening: "Poe and Mrs. Whitman sat across the room from each other. . . . All were drawn toward Poe, whose eyes were gleaming and whose utterance was most eloquent. His eyes were fixed on Mrs. Whitman. . . . Of a sudden the company perceived that Poe and Helen were greatly agitated. Simultaneously both arose from their chairs and walked toward the center of the room. Meeting, he held her in his arms, kissed her; they stood for a moment, then he led her to her seat. There was a dead silence through all this strange proceeding."[2] As well there might be, for what could one say? A kiss under such public circumstances was a virtual betrothal announcement.

The following day, Poe proposed—and was refused. Mrs. Whitman was to say, "He endeavored . . . to persuade me that my influence and my presence would have power to lift his life out of the torpor of despair which had weighed upon him, and give an inspiration to his genius. . . . Notwithstanding the eloquence with which he urged upon me his wishes and his hopes, I knew too well that I could not exercise over him the power which he ascribed to me. I was, moreover, wholly dependent on my mother, and her life was bound up in mine."[3] Mrs. Whitman's dependency was financial, and she knew her mother would disapprove a marriage to a penniless Poe and that Poe did not need a marriage to a penniless widow.

Mrs. Whitman offered Poe still more reasons for not marrying him: "You will, perhaps, attempt to convince me that my person is agreeable to you—that my countenance interests you—but in this respect I am so variable that I should inevitably disappoint you if you hoped to find in me to-morrow the same aspect which won you today."[4] How many women have felt this same way over the centuries! And, "You are not, perhaps, aware that I am many years [exactly six: they shared the same day of birth, six years apart] older than yourself. I *fear* you do not know it, and that if you *had* known it you would not have felt for me as you do." She pleaded a weak heart (she was to live to the age of seventy-five, a great age in those days of early deaths). But she also said, "I can only say to you that had I youth and health and beauty, I would live for you and die with you. Now were I to allow myself to love you, I could only enjoy a bright, brief hour of rapture and die."[5]

Poe's answer appealed to Mrs. Whitman's well-known belief in predestination and spiritual influences: ". . . as your eyes rested appealingly, for one brief moment, upon mine, I felt, for the first time in my life, and tremblingly acknowledged, the existence of spiritual influences altogether out of the reach of reason. I saw that you were *Helen*—my Helen—the Helen of a thousand dreams." This must have been hard to resist. Mrs. Whitman wrote again, using a different tack—why did so many persons speak unfavorably of him? Poe answered: "I swear to you that my soul is incapable of dishonor—that, with the exception of occasional follies and excesses which I bitterly lament, but to which I have been driven by intolerable sorrow, and which are hourly committed by others without attracting any notice whatever—I can call to mind no act of my life which would bring a blush to my cheek—or to yours." He had been slandered, he said, because of the honesty of his critiques, which have made him enemies, but: "Ah, Helen, I have a hundred friends for every individual enemy—but has it never occurred to you that you do not live *among* my friends? Miss Lynch, Miss Fuller, Miss Blackwell, Mrs.

Ellet—neither these nor any within their influence, are my friends." As for her (Mrs. Whitman's) money, ". . . under *no* circumstances, would I marry where 'interest' as the world terms it, could be suspected as, on my part, the object of the marriage."[6]

Soon after writing this letter, Poe went to see Mrs. Whitman and repeated his marriage proposal. He asked that she send her answer to Lowell, where he told her he was going to lecture. (Whether he was actually supposed to lecture or not is not known; the fact is that he *didn't*. Mrs. Whitman understood that the lecture had to be canceled because of the excitement of the imminent presidential election, but it is possible that Poe went to see Annie.)

In Lowell, Poe stayed with the Lockes, sublimely uncaring of the undercurrents swirling about in the lives of the Lockes and the Richmonds. Inevitably, however, derogatory remarks about the Richmonds surfaced in the course of conversation. Poe immediately ". . . arose & left their house & incurred the unrelenting vengeance of that worst of all fiends, 'a woman scorned.' "[7]

At the Richmond home, Poe waited to hear from Mrs. Whitman. She did not send a decisive answer, and Annie tried to advise him. The scene must have been difficult. Poe seems to have truly loved Annie, and, despite an affection for her husband, on some level Annie loved Poe (she even changed her name legally from Nancy to Annie after her husband's death). Yet there they were, trying to get him married. They both knew he needed a wife, and Mrs. Whitman was a woman of merit who could give him intellectual support (she edited "Ulalume," to rid it of the obscurities that defied even Poe). He could offer her only himself, but that was not inconsequential: he was attractive, intelligent, caring (if not loving), and one of the country's preeminent literary figures.

Poe finally went to Providence to see Mrs. Whitman, with whom he had a Sunday appointment. Poe did not keep the appointment. He went to his hotel where he wrote a letter to Annie, ". . . in which I opened my whole heart to you . . . my Annie, whom I so madly, so distractedly love. . . . I then reminded you of that holy promise . . . that . . . you would come to me on my bed of death. . . ." and swallowed half a bottle of laudanum. He took the letter to the post office, expecting to go back to the hotel and wait for Annie to come to his "bed of death" before taking the other half. But he miscalculated the strength of the laudanum, and by the time he got to the post office, his "reason was entirely gone, & the letter was never put in. . . . A friend was at hand, who aided & (if it can be called saving) saved me."[8]

Mrs. Whitman, unhappy and confused at Poe's not having kept their appointment, refused to see him when he finally arrived at her doorstep on Tuesday. She eventually agreed to meet him in a public place, the Athenaeum (the library). There, Poe told her that on Sunday he had taken laudanum to compose himself, and instead it had confused him. He had gotten on the train back to Lowell, he said, and then had to retrace the journey back to Providence. Obviously, one of these stories is not true, but whether it is the one he told Annie or the one he told Helen, we cannot be certain.

The following day, Poe saw Mrs. Whitman at her home. This time she told him that she was delaying her decision about marriage because of adverse information she had heard about him from one of Poe's associates. Poe was upset. Back at his hotel, Poe had a drink and sent Mrs. Whitman a farewell note. She was under the impression that he then returned to New York. Instead,

> he came alone to my mother's house in a state of wild & delirious excitement, calling upon me to save him from some terrible impending doom. The tones of his voice were appalling & rang through the house. Never have I heard anything so awful, even to sublimity. It was long before I could nerve myself to see him. My mother was with him more than two hours before I entered the room. He hailed me as an angel sent to save him from perdition. When my mother requested me to have a cup of strong coffee prepared for him, he clung to me so frantically as to tear away a piece of the muslin dress I wore. . . . My mother sent for [the doctor] who, finding symptoms of cerebral congestion, advised his being taken to the house of his friend Wm. J. Pabodie, where he was kindly taken care of.[9]

Some days later, Mrs. Whitman agreed to become engaged to Poe on the condition that he abstain absolutely from drinking. Years later, she was to write to John Ingram, Poe's English biographer, "If I had ever seen Poe intoxicated, I should never have consented to marry him; had he kept his promise never again to taste wine, I should never have broken the engagement." She thought she could be a power for good; she found that she had little power to control the uncontrollable.

When Mrs. Whitman's mother was informed of

the engagement, she went to her lawyers and tied up the family money in her name alone, so that Poe could not benefit from it. Mrs. Whitman sent letters to both Poe and Mrs. Clemm, her future mother-in-law, courteously and carefully outlining her new situation with regard to the estate. Poe responded, ". . . *all will go well.* My mother sends her dearest love and says she will return good for evil & treat you *much* better than *your* mother has treated me."[10] Poe, however, was not sure that all would go well, despite the lengthy correspondence they maintained. He arranged to return to Providence in December, ostensibly to lecture but also to hold on to Mrs. Whitman. Both objectives were achieved. Uplifted by the excited reception given Poe by the 2,000 or so people in the audience for his lecture, Mrs. Whitman agreed to marry Poe immediately. Her mother reluctantly consented to the union, with the proviso that Poe sign a "statement of approval and assent" to her control of the estate. Arrangements were made to post the banns for a December 25th marriage.

On the 23rd of December, Mrs. Whitman was busy preparing for her wedding when she received another warning note against Poe. (These warnings may have come through Horace Greeley and others who knew and admired Mrs. Whitman.) The note also informed her that Poe had already broken his promise—that he had taken a glass of wine at breakfast that morning at his hotel. Mrs. Whitman wrote a friend, "I felt utterly helpless of being able to exercise any permanent influence over his life."

She moved rapidly. She sent a note to the church rescinding the banns, and the marriage was off. Poe tried to dissuade her, to tell her that she had been misinformed, particularly about the morning glass of wine, but nothing would do. It is possible that Mrs. Whitman by that time was incapable of understanding what Poe was saying. She was sniffing at a handkerchief dipped in ether, a way in which some women of her time retreated from any unpleasantness with which they could not cope. Upon Poe's urging that she say something, anything, she was finally able to whisper, "I love you." At this point, her mother intervened and made Poe leave. Her mother had already said some choice things to Poe, and now he stormed out of the house "with an expression of bitter resentment at what he termed, the 'intolerable insults' of my family. I never saw him more,"[11] reminisced Poe's Helen of a Thousand Dreams.

Mrs. Clemm wrote to Annie, whom she had met some months before and liked, "I feel so happy in *all* my troubles. Eddy isn't going to marry Mrs. W.!"[12]

Perhaps Eddy was happy, too. Although he had been urging Mrs. Whitman to marry him, he was able to write this to Annie:

> So long as I think that you know I love you, as no man ever loved woman—so long as I think you comprehend in some measure, the fervor with which I adore you, so long, no worldly trouble can ever render me absolutely wretched. But oh, my darling, my Annie, my own sweet sister Annie, my pure beautiful angel—wife of my soul—to be mine hereafter and forever in the Heavens—how shall I explain to you the bitter, bitter anguish which has tortured me since I left you? [Poe tells her of his suicide attempt.] . . . I saw her [Mrs. Whitman] & spoke, for your sake, the words which you urged me

to speak [his proposal of marriage]. Ah Annie An-
nie! my Annie!—is your heart so strong? Is there no
hope!—is there none? I feel that I must die if I
persist, & yet, how can I now retract with honor?
Think—oh think of me—before the words—the vows
are spoken, which put yet another terrible bar be-
tween us. [13]

The "terrible bar" had not been raised, but that was thanks to Mrs. Whitman, not Poe or Annie. That Annie loved Poe enough to urge him to marry some-one else was confirmed in another letter, one Poe sent to Annie surreptitiously through Mrs. Clemm so that it would not be seen by other eyes: "Oh, Annie, in spite of so many worldly sorrows—in spite of all the trouble and misrepresentation (so hard to bear) that Poverty has entailed on me for so long a time—in spite of all this I am *so*—*so* happy to think that you *really* love me. . . . there is *nothing* in this world worth liv-ing for except love—love *not* such as I thought I felt for Mrs. W [Whitman] but such as burns in my very soul for *you*—so pure—so unworldly. . . ."[14]

The end to the wedding plans gave the rumor-mongers much to gossip about. They said Poe had been so drunk that he had abused Mrs. Whitman. They said that Mrs. Whitman was telling terrible things about Poe. Actually, it was the scorned Edwina Locke who was spreading vile rumors about Poe in an effort to ensure that both Mrs. Whitman and Annie were out of the way so that she could fill the void! She was pestering Mrs. Whitman, whom she did not know, with letter after letter, begging Mrs. Whitman to visit in order that she might be told confidential informa-tion about Poe. Mrs. Locke also gossiped to Annie, who was distraught. Poe sought to reassure Annie by writing to Mrs. Whitman, asking for refutation of the gossip, then enclosing the unsealed letter in a letter to Annie. Poe wanted Annie to read the letter to reassure herself of his openness in the matter, then mail it to Mrs. Whitman. Poe then planned to send Annie Mrs. Whitman's reply. Annie read the letter and mailed it, but Mrs. Whitman did not respond. She felt that a response might reopen a relationship that was better ended.

Mrs. Locke's machinations reached Annie's husband and the brother and sister who lived with the Richmonds, all of whom were fond of Poe and had accepted the caring relationship between him and Annie as an innocent one. But Mrs. Locke soon had them doubting that. Mr. Richmond, whose patience was by now sorely tried, had words with Annie. Although she made no complaint to Poe, undertones of Annie's unhappiness crept into her letters to him. Poe wrote to Annie that his only offense to Mrs. Locke's "insane vanity & self-esteem" had been to leave her home when she spoke rudely of the Richmonds and that he was not surprised that she was "ransacking the world for scandal."

But Poe was surprised that Mr. Richmond would ever listen to such a source. "God knows dear *dear* Annie, with what horror I would have shrunk from insulting a nature so divine as yours, with any impure or earthly love—But since it is clear that Mr R. cannot enter into my feelings on this topic, & that he even suspects *what is not,* it only remains for me beloved Annie to consult your happiness. . . . Not only must I *not* visit you at Lowell, but I must discontinue my letters & you yours—I cannot & *will* not have it on my conscience that I have interfered with the domestic happiness of the only being in the whole world, whom I have loved, at the same time with truth & with *purity.*"[15] By "purity," it is conjectured that Poe meant a nonsexual attraction.

Annie showed her husband the letter, which relieved his mind to the extent of his immediately issuing an invitation for Poe and Mrs. Clemm to visit. Poe responded by arranging to visit the Richmonds in Lowell. At the same time, Mrs. Whitman finally gave in to Mrs. Locke's importuning and went to visit her. But Mrs. Whitman left before Poe arrived—they found out later that their trains had passed one another—thus foiling Mrs. Locke's attempt to keep Mrs. Whitman in Lowell a while longer in order to set up a confrontation. Even as she stirred up all this mischief, Mrs. Locke continued to write gushing letters to Poe, assuring him of her continued affection. Ultimately, the thoroughly besotted woman coyly informed Poe that she planned to publish a short story based on their relationship. Poe reassured Annie that there had been no relationship other than the one that existed in Mrs. Locke's mind. Fortunately, Mrs. Locke's false story never appeared.

Poe, defeated in the north, now turned to the south—to Richmond and his former sweetheart, the widow Elmira Royster Shelton.

THE END
OF THE SEARCH
(1849)

When he returned to New York from Lowell, Poe found an almost unbelievable offer waiting for him, one that would finally allow him to publish his own magazine, the long-delayed *Stylus*. A young man from Illinois, Edward Norton Patterson, wanted to use the money he was to receive on his twenty-first birthday to start a national magazine with Poe as its sole editor. Patterson, junior editor of his father's weekly newspaper, the *Oquawka Spectator*, would act as publisher, and the two men would share profits equally.

Poe was uncharacteristically cautious about this opportunity and finally agreed to the deal only if the publication would be a "five-dollar magazine." Poe wanted the magazine to be an elegant literary publication for serious readers since that was almost twice the price of popular magazines of the day. An agreement between Patterson and Poe was finally reached, and Poe was to meet Patterson in St. Louis, where the magazine was to be published. He would travel by way of Richmond, where his new partner would send him $50 toward traveling expenses for the rest of the trip. Poe would also raise money by giving lectures at various stopovers.

There was some delay in starting out. Poe was ill. He was not drinking, so the attack cannot be laid at that doorstep. Whatever it was, Mrs. Clemm wrote to Annie that he had almost died. Poe reassured Annie that this was pure exaggeration. He was not so ill, he wrote, as he was depressed. Recent events had certainly tried him, and his search for a wife had been frustrated. Then, too, the market for his work was shrinking: this magazine was out of business, that one unable to pay for contributions, another rejecting all new articles in favor of reprints it did not have to pay for. *The Southern Literary Messenger* owed him money, and *Sartain's* and *Graham's* were shaky—*Graham's* had issued him a bank draft that had not been honored. His "Sonnet—to My Mother," written in praise of his "Muddy" rather than his real mother, and his "Landor's Cottage" were still not in print. Now for the first time Poe would have sufficient financial backing for a magazine of his own to be successful. Yet nothing in his correspondence or actions reveals any real enthusiasm over the prospect.

It was a time not unlike the one before his marriage to Virginia, when Mr. Kennedy questioned why he was allowing the blue devils to attack him just when fortune was beginning to smile on him again. But blue devils would not have warranted Mrs. Clemm's statement that he had been near death. He may have been sicker than he wanted Annie to know.

Whether it was the illness brought on by depression or depression brought on by illness, Poe was feeling uneasy about his health. According to Mrs. Clemm, he made arrangements that should he die, Rufus W. Griswold was to be his literary executor and Nathaniel P. Willis was to be his biographer and "vindicate his memory." We have only Mrs. Clemm's word for this: The written instructions she claimed Poe left her were never found, and many biographers have doubted her veracity. Griswold was no friend of Poe's, so why choose him? The answer might be that Griswold was preeminent in the field of anthology and therefore would not have been too illogical a choice.

By the end of June, Poe was well enough to start on his lecture tour to St. Louis. Mrs. Clemm and Mr. and Mrs. Lewis saw him off in a teary scene of farewell. Well might it have been tearful, for they were never to see him again.

Poe's first stop was Philadelphia, where he got separated from his trunk. What happened next is as bizarre a mystery as any that Poe himself might have written. He is said to have gotten drunk, although he stated in a letter to Mrs. Clemm that this was not so. Poe believed that he was arrested and kept in Moyamensing, the Philadelphia County Prison. Many years later, John Sartain, the engraver and publisher who saw Poe at this time, gave several different accounts of what took place and confused names, places, and dates. Essentially, Sartain denied that Poe was imprisoned in Moyamensing and said that he had merely been detained for a few hours for drunkenness, pending a hearing at the mayor's office. (Why the mayor of Philadelphia should have jurisdiction over the disposition of light offenders such as drunkards or disturbers of the peace is unknown.) Sartain said that the mayor recognized Poe and quickly dismissed whatever charge had been brought against him. But the mayor Sartain named was not the mayor of Philadelphia at this time.

The next day, Sartain said, Poe came to his home, haggard and frightened, begging for asylum from some men who were trying to kill him. Sartain, of course, admitted him. After a long silence, Poe suddenly said, as Sartain remembered his words, "If this mustache of mine were removed I should not be so readily recognized; will you lend me a razor, that I may shave it off?" Sartain never shaved and had no razor, but he offered to take the mustache off with scissors. This accomplished, Poe seemed relieved.

That evening, the two men walked by the Schuykill River and up the stairs to the reservoir, as Poe described the visions he believed he had in Moyamensing. One vision was of Mrs. Clemm being dismembered, the memory of which threw Poe into "a sort of convulsion." Sartain too had a vision—of Poe in his frenzy throwing himself into the water below, taking Sartain with him. "I suggested at last that . . . we might as well go down again. He agreed, and we descended the steep stairway slowly and cautious[ly], holding well to the hand-rails. . . . I got him safe home, and gave him a bed on a sofa in the dining-room, while I slept alongside him on three chairs, without undressing."[1]

(Could this have been the same mysterious illness that had assailed Poe in Fordham the month before, and even before that? We have no way of knowing with any certainty, but somehow it fits with Poe's description to Annie of having suffered "depression," possibly a euphemism for mania, and Mrs. Clemm's assertion that he had been near death.)

In a day or so, Poe was better and able to leave Sartain's home. He was convinced that he had suffered from hallucinations, and he wrote this harrowing note to Mrs. Clemm: "I have been *so* ill—have had the cholera, or spasms quite as bad, and can now hardly hold the pen. . . . The very instant you get this, *come* to me. The joy of seeing you will almost compensate for our sorrows. We can but die together. It is no use to reason with me *now*; I must die. I have no desire to live since I have done 'Eureka' [his treatise on cosmology]. . . . You have been all in all to me, darling, ever beloved mother, and dearest, truest friend. . . ."[2]

Poe enclosed the note in an envelope addressed to Mrs. Lewis with the admonition, "Give the enclosed *speedily* to my darling mother. It might get into the wrong hands." It would seem that Poe's paranoid delusions were still operating, if that is what they were. In a way, the letter did get into the wrong hands, for Mrs. Lewis did not forward it to Mrs. Clemm. Sensing that word from her Eddy had gone astray, Mrs. Clemm traveled to the Brooklyn home of the Lewises, and only then was she given the letter. By then, she had no idea of where Poe was, and, even if she were able to track him down, she did not have the money to get to him.

Poe was still in Philadelphia. He was starving, lacked the fresh clothing he needed from his still-lost trunk, and living on the street. He finally went to the editor of *The Quaker City*, George Lippard, for help. Lippard solicited funds for Poe, going "from door to door, but everybody was out of town. It was a wretched day; cholera bulletins upon every newspaper door, and a hot sun pouring down over half deserted streets."[3] Not until the next day was Lippard able to get a few dollars each from Sartain, Godey, and another publisher. Sartain's clerk gave "all he had—a dollar." Lippard and a friend persuaded Poe to wait at the friend's home until the train south left at ten that night. When he got to the depot, Poe found his trunk, but it had been opened, and the manuscripts for his two lectures, "The Poets and Poetry of America" and "The Poetic Principle," were gone. Had Poe really been followed and his work stolen?

Poe arrived in Richmond on the 14th of July and wrote immediately to Mrs. Clemm. "All my object here [lecturing] is over unless I can recover [the manuscripts] or re-write one of them. . . . I got here with two dollars over—of which I inclose you one. Oh God, my Mother, shall we ever again meet? If possible, oh COME! My clothes are *so horrible.* . . . Write instantly."[4] Mrs. Clemm responded quickly, for five days later Poe wrote, "Oh, if you only knew how your dear letter comforted me! It acted like magic. Most of my suffering arose from that terrible idea which I could not get rid of—the idea that you were dead. For more than ten days I was totally deranged, although I was not drinking one drop, and during this interval I imagined the most horrible calamities. . . . All was hallucination, arising from an attack which I had never before experienced—an attack of [delirium tremens]. May heaven grant that it prove a warning to me for the rest of my days. . . ."[5]

It is doubtful that Poe's diagnosis was correct; this psychotic episode was not brought on by drinking and does not have the other earmarks of delirium tremens—the "d.t.s."—but knowing that Poe occasionally had trouble with alcohol made this a convenient diagnosis for everyone, including himself. (It has been estimated that in his entire life, Poe drank what the average American executive might consume at business luncheons over a six-month period.)

Poe's stay in Richmond as compared to Philadelphia was like bright sunshine after a stormy night. The nightmare was over, and life was attractive and rewarding. Poe visited his sister Rosalie, who was delighted at the chance to show him off. Rosalie had visited her brother only two or three times in adulthood, and Poe does not seem to have had any real feeling for her. Rosalie, on the other hand, was very proud of her brother's fame. She introduced him to a friend, Susan Archer Talley, who was a poet he admired. Years later, Talley reminisced: "As I entered the parlor, Poe was seated near an open window, quietly conversing. His attitude was easy and graceful, with one arm lightly resting upon the back of his chair. His dark curling hair was thrown back from his broad forehead—a style in which he habitually wore it. . . . The impression produced upon me was of a refined, high-bred, and chivalrous gentleman. . . . He rose at my entrance, and, other visitors being present, stood with one hand resting on the back of his chair, awaiting my greeting. So dignified was his manner, so reserved his expression, that I experienced an involuntary recoil, until I turned to him and saw his eyes suddenly brighten as I offered my hand; a barrier seemed to melt between us, and I felt that we were no longer strangers."[6] Poe seems to have had this effect on many women.

Poe's visit to Richmond was not merely a stopover on the way to St. Louis—if he had any intention of ever going to that city to meet with Patterson. He had told Mrs. Clemm early on that he would attempt to make a marriage with his former sweetheart, Elmira Royster Shelton. Mrs. Clemm had written to Annie, ". . . if Eddy gets to Richmond safely and can succeed in what he intends doing, we will be relieved of part of our difficulties; but if he comes home in trouble and sick, I know not what is to become of us."[7]

Poe was an ardent suitor, but Mrs. Shelton was not overly responsive. Sometime around the end of July, he proposed marriage, and Mrs. Shelton remembered that she had responded by telling him that she was going to church and "that I never let anything interfere with that, that he must call again and when he did call again he renewed his addresses. I laughed at it, he looked very serious and I became serious. I told him if he would not take a positive denial he must give me time to consider of it—and he said a love that hesitated was not a love for him. But he sat there a long time and was very pleasant and cheerful. He continued to visit me frequently."[8] The two were together so much that reports of an engagement were beginning to circulate.

While he waited for Mrs. Shelton to make up her mind, Poe lectured in Richmond and in Norfolk on "The Poetic Principle," the notes for which he was apparently able to reconstruct. A member of the audience later commented, "The lecturer [Poe] stood in a graceful attitude, leaning one hand on a small table beside him, and his wonderfully clear and musical voice speedily brought the audience under its spell. Those who heard this strange voice once, never afterwards forgot it. It was certainly unlike any other that I have ever listened to: and the exquisite, if objectionable 'sing-song,' as he repeated, 'The Raven,' [Thomas] Hood's 'Fair Inez,' and other verse, resembled music."[9] Poe made enough to pay his room bill, with $2 left over. That left nothing to send to Mrs.

Clemm, who had to resort to begging money from acquaintances.

Poe had suffered another attack of illness, which Susan Archer Talley, writing some years later when she was Mrs. Weiss, ascribed to drink. Her *Home Life of Poe* is considered inaccurate and fanciful, so we must lend credence to Poe's statement that this sickness was cholera and its "long-continued consequences in debility and congestion of the brain." Cholera was omnipresent, but people also called any severe intestinal upset cholera in those days. Still, Poe joined the Sons of Temperance, an early version of Alcoholics Anonymous, when he recovered.

Poe wrote to Mrs. Clemm, "I spent last evening with [Elmira]. I think she loves me more devotedly than any one I ever knew & I cannot help loving her in return."[10] This was a very strange thing to say considering the love Virginia bore him, and to say it to Virginia's mother seems utterly out of keeping. But Poe, now thirty-nine years old, behaved like an adolescent about love.

Elmira Shelton was having difficulty in saying yes to Poe, probably because her late husband's will penalized her for remarrying. She stood to lose control of the very considerable estate he had left her and would receive only one-fourth of the income it generated. Although this was still a comfortable amount of money, it certainly represented a sacrifice.

Around the end of September, Poe wrote to Mrs. Clemm to tell her that Mrs. Shelton had finally said yes and that Mrs. Clemm would always have a secure home with them. He briefly outlined the financial arrangements involved and explained that he would undertake the education of Mrs. Shelton's son, then ten years old, for which he would be compensated by the estate. Mrs. Shelton wrote to Mrs. Clemm at the same time, "Mr. Poe has been very solicitous that I write to you and I do assure you, it is with emotions of pleasure that I now do so—I am fully prepared to *love* you, and I do sincerely hope that our spirits may be congenial. . . . I have just spent a very happy evening with your dear Edgar, and I know it will be gratifying to you to know that he is all that you could desire him to be, sober, temperate, moral, & much beloved. . . . Edgar speaks frequently & very affectionately of your daughter & his Virginia, for which I love him but the more."[11]

Poe now prepared to return to New York to wind up his affairs in Fordham and bring Mrs. Clemm back to Richmond. On the way he planned to stop at Philadelphia to edit the poems of a Mrs. Loud, whose husband offered him $100 for the commission. On the 24th of September, Poe lectured one more time. On the 25th, he took leave of friends and Rosalie, and it is thought that on the 26th he went to Mrs. Shelton to say goodbye. He had a fever and complained of feeling sick, but said he did not want to delay his leave-taking. He went to a nearby doctor for medication, had a late dinner at a restaurant, and was said to have been escorted by friends to the steamer leaving for Baltimore. What happened then is another Poe mystery—the greatest one.

The boat left as scheduled at 4:00 A.M. on the 27th of September and arrived on the 28th. Whether Poe was on it has never been documented. The favored explanation of his next days is that he was "cooped"—drugged and taken from polling place to polling place to cast repeated votes in the statewide October 3rd election. But what about the days between the alleged arrival date of September 28th and the election? Or did he really arrive in Baltimore after the election, on October 5th, as other explanations have it? Virtually every day in Poe's adult life has been accounted for except for these last days.

A typesetter, Joseph W. Walker, was said to have recognized Poe in a tavern. Knowing that Poe was a friend of Dr. Joseph Evans Snodgrass, a physician and once the publisher of the defunct *Saturday Visiter,* Walker sent him a message that Poe was in need of help. Snodgrass, in his version of the story some seven years later, said that Poe called for him by name, and someone came to his home to get him. Dr. Snodgrass went to the tavern and found Poe in a drunken stupor, wearing cheap, dirty clothes that didn't fit and a badly soiled, torn palm-leaf hat. Dr. Snodgrass was an avid temperance man who saw Poe's state as the sad but just fate of the drinker, and he made no attempt to determine if Poe was ill rather than drunk. Snodgrass said he ordered a room at the tavern until Poe's relatives could be sent for, but they, having been informed somehow, entered at just that moment and decided that they could not have him in their homes in that condition and sent him to the hospital instead. Whether hospitalization took place on the 3rd, the 4th, or the 6th of October is debatable in view of conflicting stories.

At any rate, Poe was admitted to Washington College Hospital and he died there at 5:00 A.M. on Sunday, the 7th of October, 1849. He was forty years old.

Poe's uncle by marriage, Henry Herring, and his cousin, Neilson Poe, were said to have arranged for

Poe to be buried in the Presbyterian graveyard where his grandparents and brother Henry were buried. The resident physician who had treated Poe at the hospital, Dr. John J. Moran, contacted the Rev. William T. D. Clemm, a distant relative of Virginia's, to perform the burial service. The funeral took place on the day following Poe's death, without anyone notifying Mrs. Clemm or any of Poe's friends who would have wanted to be there. Why? This is another Poe mystery.

Annie Richmond learned of Poe's death from the newspapers. She wrote to Mrs. Clemm:

> Oh my mother, my darling darling mother oh what shall I say to you—how can I comfort you. . . . Oh if I could only have laid down my life for his, that he might have been spared to you—but mother it is the will of God, and we must submit, and Heaven grant us strength, to bear it. . . . Your letter [written on the 9th, just after Mrs. Clemm heard—we do not know how—of Poe's death] has this moment reached me, but I had seen a notice of his death, a few moments previous in the paper—oh mother, when I read it, I said no, no it is not true my Eddie can't be dead, no, it is not so I could not believe it, until I got your letter. . . . My own heart is breaking, and I cannot offer you consolation that I would now, but mother, I will pray for you, and for myself, that I may be able to comfort you—Mr. R. [her husband] begs that you will come on here, soon as you can, and stay with us long as you please—Do dear mother, gather up all his papers and books, and take them and come to your own Annie. [12]

Annie recognized the value of those papers and books.

Mrs. Shelton also wrote to Mrs. Clemm several days after Poe's death. "The pleasure I anticipated on his return with you, dear friend! to Richmond, was too great ever to have been realized, and should teach me the folly of expecting bliss on earth,"[13] but she was to deny to all the world that they ever planned marriage. She was probably embarrassed by the onerous things said about Poe.

The Reverend Clemm recalled that the only people at the funeral besides himself, were Poe's uncle, Henry Herring, with his daughter, Elizabeth, and her husband, Edmund Morton Smith, Dr. Snodgrass, Neilson Poe, Z. Collins Lee (a college classmate of Poe's), Joseph H. Clarke (Poe's teacher when he was a young boy), the church sexton, and the undertaker. Mr. Herring said that he paid for the coffin, and Neilson Poe had paid for the hearse and the cost of a carriage to the cemetery. Neilson said, too, that he provided a small monument for the grave, but it broke before it could be set up and was replaced by a simple marker bearing nothing but the plot number, 80. The service was described by a bystander as "not occupy-[ing] more than three minutes . . . [and] so cold-blooded . . . as to provoke on my part a sense of anger difficult to suppress. . . . In justice to the people of Baltimore I must say that if the funeral had been postponed for a single day, until the death was generally known, a far more imposing escort to the tomb and one more worthy of the many admirers of the poet in the city would have taken place."[14] And perhaps Poe's friends and loved ones could have been there.

A poet and editor, Charles William Hubner, remembered how, as a boy of fourteen, he had passed by the hospital just as Poe's casket was being put into the hearse. He asked one of the men attending it who they were going to bury. The man replied, "My son, that is the body of a great poet, Edgar Allan Poe; you will learn all about him some day."[15]

A GROTESQUE TALE (1849 On)

Death did not end Edgar Allan Poe's story. Indeed, death seemed to make him more visible to the world as his works grew in popularity and details of his life and death were told, refuted, obscured, and retold time and again until fact and fiction were irretrievably melded into one.

Dr. Snodgrass's account of finding Poe stuporous in a tavern was radically changed in later years. Both he and Poe had been "cooped," he said. He had survived the ordeal only because of his superior constitution, but Poe's poor physical condition had not withstood the drugging to which they were subjected.

Dr. Moran, the physician who tended Poe on his deathbed, also told two very different stories over the years. The first was written some five weeks after Poe died and was in response to a letter from Mrs. Clemm asking for details of her Eddy's last hours. Dr. Moran told her that Poe had been either unconscious or incoherent most of the time—several days—and that he had been able to question Poe only during his few brief moments of lucidity. Poe had spoken of a wife in Richmond (possibly confusing his impending marriage to Elmira as already having taken place), his lost trunk, and, according to Dr. Moran, his misery at having "sunk to the depths" once again. He lapsed a final time into delirium, and for hours called out the name "Reynolds." At about 3:00 A.M. he became quiet, Dr. Moran wrote, and, "Gently moving his head he said 'Lord help my poor Soul' and expired!"[1]

Many Poe experts believe that Poe, not a religious man, never said these last words, and that Moran inserted them for Mrs. Clemm's sake. And in later years, Dr. Moran wrote quite a different version of Poe's last words: "The dying man then said impressively, 'He who arched the heavens and upholds the universe, has His decrees legibly written upon the frontlet of every human being, and upon demons incarnate." This is far less creditable than the first version—not just that Poe said it, but that the doctor could possibly have remembered such an oration.

Dr. Moran made still more contradictory and confusing statements in his book, *A Defense of Edgar Allan Poe: Life, Character, and Dying Declarations of the Poet. An Official Account of his Death, by His Attending Physician,* published in 1885. In this version of Poe's last days, Dr. Moran wrote that Poe was in his care for only sixteen hours and that he was "sensible and rational fifteen hours out of the sixteen. He answered promptly and correctly all questions asked, spoke freely, and made certain statements, and gave certain directions to whom I should write . . . and their answers to my letters after his death came speedily and are with me now." Dr. Moran said Poe was admitted to the hospital on October 6th at about 9:00 A.M. and died between twelve and one o'clock on the 7th. He stated, "I have the evidence and the proof from Mrs. Shelton, his affianced, that the poet parted from her at her residence at 4:00 P.M. October 4th." If this were so, Poe could not have been "cooped," since he would have arrived in Baltimore on the 5th, after the election.

Dr. Moran stated that on evidence from the train's engineer, Captain George W. Rollins, Poe had taken the train for Philadelphia about noon on the 5th of October. In those days, passengers had to disembark from the train and cross the Susquehanna River by ferry, but on the 5th a storm had made the crossing impossible. Poe had gone back to Baltimore. Captain Rollins told Dr. Moran, and supposedly Poe's cousin Neilson, that he had taken particular note of Poe, whose face was known to him, because some thugs appeared to be following him. The next morning, someone found Poe unconscious on a wharf and recognized him despite the rags in which he was clothed. This unknown person had called a hack (cab) and gave the driver a card on which he wrote Dr. Moran's address and the name *POE* in the lower-right-hand corner. The driver of the hack was said to have affirmed Dr. Moran's statement that Poe was not drunk and that there was no smell of liquor about him.

In his book, Dr. Moran stated categorically that Poe had not died of alcoholism. He told of a visit to Poe by Professor J.C.S. Monkur, who "gave it as his opinion that Poe would die from excessive nervous prostration and loss of nerve power, resulting from exposure, affecting the encephalon, a sensitive and delicate membrane of the brain." Originally, Dr. Moran had written to Mrs. Clemm that Poe had died of delirium tremens, and he made no attempt to explain this or other inconsistencies in his stories.

Moran also refuted the statement by Neilson Poe that he had been turned away from visiting the delirious patient, but that he had sent over fresh clothing for Poe. Dr. Moran wrote: "I take this opportunity to assert that both statements are utterly untrue and without the slightest foundation." Not only had Nielson never attempted to visit, Moran said, but he also never sent any clothes to his cousin. Moran named students at the hospital who had donated clothing from their own wardrobe for Poe to be buried in. Nor had Mr. Herring provided Poe's coffin, as had been claimed. Moran wrote that he ordered and paid for the coffin, and the doctor offered a witnessed statement to that effect from the undertaker.

Dr. Moran had a different view also of Poe's funeral, which, he said, was attended by the mayor of Baltimore and other luminaries, as well as professors and students from the hospital. Poe's body had lain in state in the rotunda of the hospital so that Baltimoreans could pay their respects. At least fifty women were given locks of Poe's hair as a remembrance.

There is no mention in Dr. Moran's book of Poe's calling for a "Reynolds." Biographers, who almost unanimously prefer Dr. Moran's early letter to his much later and obviously flawed book, worry about who Reynolds was and what he meant to Poe. The only known Reynolds in Poe's life was the explorer who inspired him to write his novel, *The Adventures of Arthur Gordon Pym.* Someone uncovered a typesetter by that name whom Poe might have known, and one of the candidates in the Baltimore election in 1849 was named Reynolds, but these are unlikely candidates, they fret. (These biographers ignore the fact that the name may never have been spoken.)

If the people who knew Poe in life and death made such contradictory statements, how can we know what is true and what is not? We can't. We can only piece together a clue here, a guess there, a feeling. . . .

Despite the fact that so much has been written about Poe, his life remains a mystery shrouded in a welter of fictions and selective interpretations, both pro and con. Poe himself confused the facts. He had "a morbid love of mystification, as had Byron." He used several dates of birth, and said different things at different times about the years he spent in the army under an assumed name. Writers who cannot reconcile Poe with military service still choose to offer other explanations for those years despite compelling data from official records. And encyclopedias in Russia still document as fact Poe's story of his visit to that country, although it has been generally conceded that Poe was never there. Nor had he been to any other place on the European continent, yet, as he lay seriously ill after Virginia's death, he had Mrs. Shew write down the details of a duel he insisted he had fought in Paris. He even showed her a scar on his shoulder to prove it. Perhaps . . . maybe . . . it *could* have happened . . . and reality and unreality trade places.

Careful and extensive study can yield clear-cut evidence about most dates and places in Poe's life, but the more subjective issues of character and personality were irremediably tainted after Poe's death.

Horace Greeley asked Rufus Griswold to write an obituary on Poe for the *New York Daily Tribune*. Written over a pseudonym, "Ludwig," the obituary was nasty, vindictive, and distorted. It was picked up by many newspapers around the country, and soon it was regarded as the truth about Poe. Friends of Poe—John Neal, George R. Graham, and Nathaniel P. Willis—

published denials of the Ludwig article. Griswold responded by writing an even more virulent "Memoir" in his 1850 edition of Poe's works. He stooped to forgery as well, adding laudatory remarks about himself and incriminating material on Poe.

Enemies like Thomas Dunn English and Mrs. Ellet hastened to stab the corpse. Poe was a drunkard, an opium addict, a madman, a necrophile, a pedophile, a lecher, a philanderer, a liar, a cheat, a blackmailer . . . . Readers felt that the allegations had to be true, for why would anyone want to lie about such things? But people did lie. Friends of Poe tried to defend him, but damage as extensive as this could not—and cannot—be completely repaired. Refutation also demanded restatement of the falsehoods and helped perpetuate them—to this very day.

Why did Poe pick Griswold, whom he knew was not his friend, to be his literary executor? If he had, Poe could certainly not have anticipated that Griswold hated him so that he would defame him and at the same time profit from the publication of his work. But we can't be sure that Poe did choose him. Griswold and Mrs. Clemm said he did, but they may have concocted that story themselves. Mrs. Clemm felt that Poe's material belonged to her, and she expected Griswold to give her a share of the profits. (Several sources call the 1850 edition of Poe's collected works "Mrs. Clemm's edition," even though it contained the defamatory memoir.) But Mrs. Clemm said that she never received anything more than a few copies to peddle where she could, although some people say she received a small annual income from the publishers.

Poe's writings benefited his "Muddy" very little. For the rest of her life, Mrs. Clemm depended on the charity of Poe's friends. Sarah Helen Whitman gave her money despite the fact that she was aware of Mrs. Clemm's dislike; Annie and her husband, Stella Lewis and her husband, Mrs. Marie Louise Shew Houghton, and others gave Mrs. Clemm room and board over the years. Charles Dickens gave her $150 when he made his second visit to the United States; Walt Whitman and other writers and editors also gave her money, often because she begged for it. People's patience with Mrs. Clemm always seemed to wear out, and she would have to find new refuges. Marie Louise Shew Houghton was infuriated with her for not returning her (Mrs. Houghton's) letters to Poe, probably because she was afraid they would be published, but Mrs. Clemm had burned them along with every other woman's letters to Poe. (Unfortunately for biographers, she also chose to burn the letter from Mrs. Allan that Virginia had shown on her deathbed to Mrs. Shew Houghton as well as the packet of letters Elizabeth Poe had given to the two-year-old Edgar.)

Mrs. Lewis accused Mrs. Clemm of interfering between her and her husband before their divorce. We do not know what happened between Mrs. Clemm and Annie, but this shelter also evaporated. Mrs. Clemm moved to Ohio at the invitation of a Poe admirer and would-be biographer, Sallie Elizabeth Robins. But Sallie Robins went mad (one of Poe's biographers commented ruefully that trying to understand Poe's life could do that!), and Mrs. Clemm found herself stranded in Ohio in the middle of the Civil War. Resourceful woman that she always was, she managed to find her way back east despite the chaotic wartime conditions. She spent her last years in a Baltimore charitable institution, the Episcopal

Church Home, and died there. The home had once been the Washington College Hospital, where her Eddy had died. She was buried beside him.

Rosalie Mackenzie Poe also spent the last years of her life in dire poverty—her money and that of the Mackenzie family evaporated with the Confederacy at the end of the Civil War. As her brother's closest relative, she tried to gain possession of his increasingly valuable manuscripts and the portrait of her mother from Mrs. Clemm and others, but she was unsuccessful. For a while, she tried to support herself by selling likenesses of her brother on the streets of Richmond and Baltimore. She finally gained admission into the Epiphany Church Home for the poor in Washington, D.C. The home did not seem to provide her with anything more than shelter, for many who saw her in those years remarked on her wearing the same thin dress winter and summer.

Poe's English biographer, John Ingram (who had Elizabeth Poe's portrait and had no intention of sending it to her daughter Rosalie), said he was enlisting subscriptions to help Rosalie, but he was always too busy or too incapacitated by one illness or another to collect much money before she died. Friends of Poe said that they gave Rosalie money but that she was improvident with it—sheltered all her life by the Mackenzies, she probably had no idea of how to handle money. Or perhaps they never gave enough money for her to survive, as John Allan had not given enough to her brother.

Mrs. Shelton managed to weather the Civil War but not the furor raised by Poe biographers. She refused to talk to any of them about Poe and denied that the two had been engaged to marry, admitting only to an "understanding" between them. Late in her life, she gave a single interview to Edward Valentine, who was acting for John Ingram. She also must have spoken for several hours to Dr. Moran, whose book defended Poe's reputation and was written to please her, not to mention to satisfy the doctor's desire to identify with the very famous man Poe had become.

Of all Poe's women, it was Sarah Helen Whitman who defended him the most passionately. Frances Sargent Osgood had inserted a weak defense into Griswold's "Memoirs," which was certainly not the forum in which to plead for Poe's reputation. She might have done more had she lived, but she died of consumption the year following Poe's death. Mrs. Whitman had been more afraid of Griswold than Mrs. Osgood was. Griswold's strong personality and power in the literary world intimidated her, but she grew less timid with age and worked hard after Griswold's death to retrieve Poe's reputation. (Griswold's reputation by then was in even worse condition: He had married for money, and when he found a wealthier woman, he had obtained a fraudulent divorce and married the second woman bigamously. Mrs. Ellet, who had hounded the Poes with her lies, turned with relish to Griswold, torturing everyone concerned, guilty and innocent, by spreading the truth.)

Mrs. Whitman did not have access to Poe's originals to compare with Griswold's distorted material (this has since been done). But the evidence she did have went far to disprove many slanderous allegations. She wrote numerous articles and a well-received book, *Edgar Poe and His Critics*, published in 1860. She also rendered great assistance to the many biographers who sought her out after the tempestuous days of the Civil War had quieted down.

In particular, she befriended and assisted Poe's English biographer, John Ingram, over a period of years. He repaid her kindness and assistance at the end by keeping some of her materials and by suggesting that she had not been entirely truthful with him. He preferred to believe some conflicting—and inaccurate—stories. Worse, he spitefully published the love letters Poe had written to Annie Richmond while courting Mrs. Whitman, although Annie had expressly forbidden him to do so. For all those years, Poe's Helen of a Thousand Dreams had thought she had been the only woman Poe had loved beside "his Virginia." Ingram destroyed that precious memory maliciously and publicly. She responded as publicly with an intelligent, witty reprimand of Ingram, defending Poe's honor to the end—she died a few months afterward.

Despite the turmoil—or perhaps aided by it—Poe's reputation as a poet and writer of fiction lived on and grew to heroic proportions. In France, his reputation equals that of Shakespeare, promoted by the great writers Baudelaire and Mallarmé. Edouard Manet and great artists around the world have illustrated his works. In Japan, Poe is the revered Edogawa Rampo (a transliteration into English of how his name is pronounced in Japanese). Poe's work is part of the literature of virtually every country in the world. But in the United States Poe's true role in literary history is not fully appreciated. It was his very bad luck that in death his name would be sullied by Griswold and others, and that their defamation would gain credence

among the American reading public and affect its judgment of his work.

Gaily bedight,
A gallant knight,
In sunshine and in shadow,
Had journeyed long,
Singing a song,
In search of Eldorado.

But he grew old—
This knight so bold—
And o'er his heart a shadow
Fell as he found
No spot of ground
That looked like Eldorado.

And, as his strength
Failed him at length,
He met a pilgrim shadow—
"Shadow," said he,
"Where can it be—
This land of Eldorado?"

"Over the Mountains
Of the moon,
Down the Valley of the Shadow,
Ride, boldly ride,"
The shade replied,—
"If you seek for Eldorado."

This poem, "Eldorado," was probably Edgar Allan
Poe's last. Poe did not find his Eldorado in life, but
perhaps over the mountains of the moon and down the
Valley of the Shadow, he found peace.

. . . The old Presbyterian cemetery saw its share of burials, and gradually filled as the city of Baltimore grew large in the decades following Poe's death. The Civil War worked its evils, then was over, and the city settled down to normalcy. The grave marked number 80 did not change, did not bear a name or dates to tell the world about the man who lay there. Then, in the early 1870s, a Baltimore schoolteacher, Miss S. S. Rice, started a campaign to raise funds for a monument to commemorate the life and death of Edgar Allan Poe. Thousands of schoolchildren donated their pennies, and people who enjoyed Poe's gifts gave to him in turn.

Poe's coffin was dug up to allow the monument to be set. Falling apart, the coffin was placed inside a bronze vault for reburial, but not before it was opened by curiosity seekers who reported that the skeleton was intact and the skull still had hair on it. A few teeth were lying around loose in the coffin. The remains were supposedly left undisturbed, although small pieces of the coffin found their way into pockets as souvenirs. (They fetch a handsome sum of money on the collectors' market to this day.)

Finally, the monument was placed, the ceremonies took place. Aside from Walt Whitman, no famed poets were there. They did not approve of what they knew of Poe, but what they knew they had learned from contaminated sources like Griswold.

One of Poe's more sympathetic biographers, William F. Gill, went to Fordham to find Virginia Poe's grave, but it was no longer there. The cemetery had been destroyed to make way for the growing city. The old caretaker had saved her bones, however, and brought them to Gill on a shovel. The appalled Gill put them in a box and kept them in his home—reportedly under his bed—until they could be reburied next to those of her husband.

It is a horror story beyond the imagination of even an Edgar Allan Poe.

CHRONOLOGY OF COMPOSITION AND PUBLICATION DATES OF POEMS AND TALES

(Adapted from *The Life of Edgar Allan Poe: Personal and Literary* by George E. Woodberry, published 1909 by Houghton Mifflin Company, Boston and New York. While later research shifted some dates about slightly, Woodberry's bibliography is unparalleled.)

Titles in parentheses are later titles.
Key to abbreviations:
> Y.L.G.—The Yankee and Boston Literary Gazette
> B.J.–Broadway Journal (no dates; vol. numbers instead)
> G.M.–Burton's Gentleman's Magazine
> A.C.–Atkinson's Philadelphia Casket
> S.L.M.–Southern Literary Messenger
> S.M.–Saturday Museum
> S.C.–Saturday Courier
> Gra.M.–Graham's Magazine
> A.W.R.–American Whig Review
> Pio.–The Pioneer
> S.V.–Baltimore Saturday Visiter
> S.E.P.–Philadelphia Saturday Evening Post
> God. L.B.–Godey's Lady's Book
> A.M.–Baltimore American Museum
> A. Mo.–American Monthly
> E.M.–New York Evening Mirror
> M.M.–Missionary Memorial
> H.J.–Home Journal
> C.M.–Columbian Magazine

U.M.–Union Magazine
S.U.M.–Sartain's Union Magazine
F.U.–Flag of Our Union
N.Y.T.–New York Tribune
Gris.–Griswold's edition of *Poets and Poetry of America, 1842*
S.L.C.–Snowden's Lady's Companion (Publication of poems in the editions of 1827, 1829, 1831, and 1845 and publication of tales in the editions of 1840, 1843, and 1845 are indicated by those dates only.)

POEMS

1. Tamerlane. 1827; extracts in Y.L.G. 1829; 1829; 1831; 1845.

2. Song (I saw thee on thy bridal day). (To _____) 1827; 1829; B.J. ii,11; 1845.

3. Dreams. 1827.

4. Spirits of the Dead. (Visit of the Dead) 1827; 1829; G.M. 1839.

5. Evening Star. 1827.

6. A Dream Within A Dream. (Imitation) 1827; extract in Y.L.G. 1829; (To _____) 1829; incorporated in Tamerlane 1831. The title is Griswold's.

7. Stanzas (No title) 1827.

8. A Dream (No title) 1827; B.J. ii,6; 1845.

9. No title (first line "The happiest day, the happiest hour") 1827.

10. The Lake. (To _____) 1827; 1829; incorporated in Tamerlane 1831 but not in 1845; M.M. 1846.

11. Alone, written into a young lady's album on March 17, 1829; published in Scribner's Magazine 1875.

12. To Science. No title in 1829; (Sonnet—To Science in subsequent publications.) A.C. 1830; 1831; S.L.M. 1836; B.J. ii, 4; 1845.

13. Al Aaraaf. 1829. Extracts in Y.L.G. 1829; 1831; extracts in S.M. 1843; 1845.

14. To _____. ("The bowers whereat in dreams I saw") 1829; B.J. ii,11; 1845.

15. To the River _____. 1829; G.M. 1839; S.M. 1843; B.J.;

1845. (Poe meant for readers to understand he meant Italy's River Po, a play on his name. Few did.)

16. To ____. ("I heed not that my earthly lot") (To M ____) 1829; 1845.

17. Fairyland. Extract in Y.L.G. 1829; 1829; 1831; G.M. 1839; B.J. ii,13; 1845.

18. Romance. (Preface) 1829; (Introduction) 1831; S.M. 1843; B.J. ii,13; 1845.

19. To Helen. 1831; S.L.M. 1836; Gra.M. 1841; S.M. 1843; 1845.

20. Israfel. 1831; S.L.M. 1836; Gra.M. 1841; S.M. 1843; B.J. ii,3; 1845.

21. The City in the Sea. (The Doomed City) 1831; (The City of Sin) S.L.M. 1835; A.W.R. 1845; B.J. ii,8; 1845.

22. The Sleeper. (Irene) 1831; S.L.M. 1836; Gris. 1842; S.M. 1843; B.J. i,18; 1845.

23. Lenore. (A Paean) 1831; S.L.M. 1836; Pio. 1843; S.M. 1843; B.J. ii,6; 1845.

24. The Valley of Unrest. (The Valley Nis) 1831; S.L.M. 1836; A.W.R. 1845; B.J. ii,6; 1845.

25. Coliseum. S.V. 1833; S.L.M. 1835; S.E.P. 1841; Gris. 1842; S.M. 1843; B.J. ii,1; 1845.

26. To One in Paradise. God.L.B. 1834; S.L.M. 1835; (To Ianthe in Heaven) G.M. 1839; Tales (in "The Visionary") 1840; S.M. 1843; B.J. (within "the Assignation")i,23; 1845.

27. Hymn. (within Morella) S.L.M. 1835; G.M. 1839; Tales 1840; B.J. i,25; (Catholic Hymn) B.J. ii,6; 1845.

28. To F____. (To Mary) S.L.M. 1835; (To One Departed) Gra.M. 1842 and S.M. 1843; B.J. ii,17; 1845.

29. To F____s S. O____d. (Lines Written in an Album) S.L.M. 1835; (To____), G.M. 1839; (To F____), B.J. ii,10; 1845.

30. Scenes from Politian (Scenes from an Unpublished Drama), S.L.M. 1835–36; 1845.

31. Bridal Ballad. S.L.M. 1837; (Ballad) S.E.P. 1841; (Song of the Newly-Wedded) S.M. 1843; B.J. ii,4; 1845.

32. To Zante. S.L.M. 1837; S.M. 1843; B.J. ii,2; 1845. Title given as Sonnet to Zante in all.

33. The Haunted Palace. A.M. 1839; untitled in "The Fall of the House of Usher" in G.M. 1839 as well as in Tales 1840; Gris. 1842; S.M. 1843; in Tales 1845; 1845.

34. Silence. (Silence. A Sonnet) G.M. 1840; (Sonnet—Silence) S.M. 1843 and B.J. ii, 3; 1845.

35. The Conqueror Worm. Gra.M. 1843; S.M. 1843; B.J. i,21; B.J. (within "Ligeia") ii,12; 1845.

36. Dreamland. Gra.M., 1844; B.J. i,26; 1845.

37. The Raven. E.M. 1845; A.W.R. 1845; B.J. i,6; S.L.M. 1845; 1845.

38. Eulalie. A.W.R. 1845; B.J. ii,5; 1845.

39. To M.L.S _____. H.J. 1847.

40. Ulalume. A.W.R. 1847; H.J. 1848. Text is Griswold 1850.

41. To_____ _____. (To _____) Addressed to Mrs. Shew—the text is in Griswold 1850.

42. An Enigma. (Sonnet.) U.M. 1848. Sent to Mrs. Lewis 1847.

43. To Helen (To _____) U.M. 1848. Text in Griswold 1850.

44. A Valentine, S.U.M. 1849; F.U. 1849. Addressed to Mrs. Osgood. Ms. dated Feb. 14, 1846.

45. For Annie, Sent to Mrs. Richmond March 23, 1849. F.U. 1849; Text is Griswold 1850.

46. To My Mother. F.U. 1849. Text is Griswold 1850.

47. Annabel Lee. N.Y.T. 1849; S.L.M. 1849; S.U.M. 1850.

48. The Bells. S.U.M. 1849.

49. Eldorado. Griswold, 1850.

The order of composition of 39–49 may be 44, 40, 39, 41, 42, 48, and 45. Dates are uncertain for 46, 47, and 49.

TALES

1. MS. Found in a Bottle. S.V. 1833; S.L.M. 1835; The Gift 1836; 1840, B.J. ii,14.

2. The Assignation (The Visionary). God.L.B. 1834; S.L.M. 1835; 1840; B.J. i,23.

3. Berenice. S.L.M., 1835; 1840; B.J. i,14.

4. Morella. S.L.M. 1835; 1840; B.J. i,25.

5. Lionizing. S.L.M. 1835; 1840; 1845; B.J. i,11.

6. Hans Pfaall. S.L.M. 1835; 1840.

7. Bon-Bon. S.L.M. 1835; 1840; B.J. i,16.

8. Shadow—A Parable (Fable). S.L.M., 1835; 1840; B.J. i,22.

9. Loss of Breath. S.C. 1831; S.L.M. 1835; 1840; B.J. ii,26.

10. King Pest. S.L.M. 1835; 1840; B.J. ii,15.

11. Metzengerstein. S.C. 1831; S.L.M. 1836; 1840.

12. Duc de L'Omelette. S.C. 1831; S.L.M. 1836; 1840; B.J. ii,14.

13. Four Beasts in One (Epimanes). S.L.M. 1836; 1840; B.J. ii,22.

14. A Tale of Jerusalem. S.C. 1831; S.L.M. 1836; 1840; B.J. ii,11.

15. Mystification (Von Jung). A.Mo. 1837; 1840; B.J. ii,25.

16. Silence—A Fable (Siope). Baltimore Book 1839; 1840; B.J. ii,9.

Numbers 1–16 made up the unpublished collection "Tales of the Folio Club."

17. Ligeia. A.M. 1838; 1840; B.J. ii,12.

18. How to Write a Blackwood Article (The Signora Zenobia). A.M. 1838; 1840; B.J. ii,1.

19. A Predicament (The Scythe of Time). A Pendant to the preceding tale. A.M. 1838; 1840; B.J. ii,1.

20. The Devil in the Belfry. The (Philadelphia) Saturday Chronicle and Mirror of the Times 1839; 1840; B.J. ii,18.

21. The Man That Was Used Up. G.M. 1839; 1840; 1843; B.J. ii,5.

22. The Fall of the House of Usher. G.M. 1839; 1840; 1845.

23. William Wilson. G.M. 1839; The Gift 1840; 1840; B.J. ii,8.

24. The Conversation of Eiros and Charmion. G.M. 1839; 1840; 1845.

25. Why the Little Frenchman Wears His Hand in a Sling. 1840; B.J. ii,9.

Tales of the Grotesque and Arabesque, 2 volumes, Philadelphia, Lea & Blanchard, 1840, was published in December 1839 and included all 25 titles listed above. Nos. 26–34 were offered later for inclusion in a second edition but were rejected.

26. The Business Man (Peter Pendulum). G.M. 1840; B.J. ii,4.

27. The Man of the Crowd. G.M. 1840; 1845.
28. The Murders in the Rue Morgue. Gra.M. 1841; 1843; 1845.
29. A Descent into the Maelström. Gra.M. 1841; 1845.
30. The Island of the Fay. Gra.M. 1841; B.J. ii,13.
31. The Colloquy of Monos and Una. Gra. M. 1841; 1845.
32. Never Bet the Devil Your Head. Gra. M. 1841; B.J. ii,6.
33. Three Sundays in a Week (A Succession of Sundays). S.E.P. 1841; B.J. i,19.
34. Eleonora. The Gift 1841; B.J. i,21.
35. The Oval Portrait (Life in Death). Gra.M. 1842; B.J. i,17.
36. The Masque of the Red Death. Gra. M. 1842; B.J. ii,2.
37. The Landscape Garden. S.L.C. 1842; B.J. ii,11. Afterward incorporated with "The Domain of Arnheim."
38. The Mystery of Marie Rogêt. S.L.C. 1842–43; 1845.
39. The Pit and the Pendulum. The Gift 1843; B.J. i,20.
40. The Tell-tale Heart. Pio. 1843; B.J. ii,7.
41. The Gold Bug. The (Philadelphia) Dollar Newspaper 1843; 1845.
42. The Black Cat. The (Philadelphia) United States Saturday Post 1843; 1845.
43. The Elk (Morning on the Wissahickon). The Opal, 1844.
44. A Tale of the Ragged Mountains. God.L.B. 1844; B.J. ii, 21.
45. The Spectacles. B.J. ii,20.
46. Diddling Considered as one of the Exact Sciences. B.J. ii, 10.
47. The Balloon Hoax. The (New York) Sun, 1844.
48. Mesmeric Revelation. C.M. 1844; 1845.
49. The Premature Burial. An unknown Philadelphia journal, August 1844; B.J. i,24.
50. The Oblong Box. God.L.B. 1844; B.J. ii,23.
51. The Angel of the Odd. C.M. 1844.
52. Thou Art the Man. God.L.B. 1844.
53. The Literary Life of Thingum-Bob. S.L.M. 1844; B.J. ii,3.
54. The Purloined Letter. The Gift 1845; 1845.

Tales, published by Wiley & Putnam, New York, 1845, included
5,22,24,27,28,29,31,38,41,42,48, and 54.

55. The System of Doctor Tarr and Professor Fether. Gra.M. 1845.

56. The Thousand and Second Tale of Scheherazade. God.L.B. 1845; B.J. ii,16.

57. Some Words with a Mummy. A.W.R. 1845; B.J. ii, 17.

58. The Power of Words. Democratic Review 1845; B.J. ii,16.

59. The Imp of the Perverse. Gra.M. 1845; Mayflower 1846.

60. The Facts in the Case of M. Valdemar. A.W.R. 1845; B.J. ii, 14.

61. The Sphinx. A.M. 1846.

62. The Cask of Amontillado. God.L.B. 1846.

63. The Domain of Arnheim. C.M. 1847.

64. Mellonta Tauta. God. L.B. 1849.

65. Hop-Frog. F.U. 1849. (Poe wrote to Annie Richmond on February 8, 1849, "The 5 prose pages I finished yesterday are called—what do you think?—I am sure you will never guess—"Hop-Frog!" Only think of *your* Eddy writing a story with *such* a name. . . . It will be published in a weekly paper [at] about 5$ a page.")

66. X-ing a Paragrab. F.U. 1849.

67. Landor's Cottage. F.U. 1849.

68. VonKempelen and His Discovery. F.U. 1849.

Printed abroad in Poe's lifetime: "The Fall of the House of Usher," "The Purloined Letter," "Mesmeric Revelation," "The Case of M. Valdemar," "Mesmerism," "The Murders in the Rue Morgue," and unspecified tales were translated into *Les Contes d'Edgar Poe* 1846.

Source Notes

CHAPTER ONE: A CHILD OF TWO WORLDS

1. Thomas, Dwight and Jackson, David Kelly, *The Poe Log*, p. 18.
2. *Ibid.*, p. 36.
3. *Ibid.*, p. 42.
4. *Ibid.*, p. 47.
5. *Ibid.*, p. 61–62.
6. *Ibid.*, p. 61.

CHAPTER TWO: CAST OUT, AND CASTING ABOUT

1. *The Poe Log*, pp. 75–76.
2. *Ibid.*, p. 84.
3. *Ibid.*, p. 86.
4. *Ibid.*, p. 90.
5. *Ibid.*, p. 98.
6. Ostrom, John Ward, ed., *The Letters of Edgar Allan Poe*, v. 1, pp. 32–33.
7. *The Poe Log*, p. 115.
8. *The Letters of Edgar Allan Poe*, v. 1, pp. 44–45.

CHAPTER THREE: WRITER AND EDITOR, SUITOR AND HUSBAND

1. *The Letters of Edgar Allan Poe*, v. 1, pp. 43–44.
2. *Ibid.*, v. 1, p. 49.
3. *The Poe Log*, p. 134.
4. *Ibid.*, p. 128.
5. *Ibid.*, p. 137 (as published in "The Richmond Standard," 7 May 1881).
6. Woodberry, George E., *The Life of Edgar Allan Poe: Personal and Literary*, v. 2, p. 443.

7. *The Letters of Edgar Allan Poe*, v. 1, p. 69 (dated 29 Aug. 1835).
8. *The Poe Log*, p. 170–71.
9. *Ibid.*, p. 170.
10. *Ibid.*, p. 240.
11. *Ibid.*, p. 241.
12. *Ibid.*, p. 236.

CHAPTER FOUR: HARDER TIMES

1. *The Poe Log*, p. 294.
2. *The Letters of Edgar Allan Poe*, v. 1, pp. 128–29.
3. *The Poe Log*, pp. 320–21.
4. *The Letters of Edgar Allan Poe*, v. 1, pp. 199–200.
5. *The Poe Log*, 329.
6. *Ibid.*, p. 358.
7. *The Letters of Edgar Allan Poe*, v.1, pp. 191–93.
8. *The Poe Log*, pp. 359–60.
9. *The Letters of Edgar Allan Poe*, v. 1, pp. 197–99.
10. *The Poe Log*, p. 368.
11. *Ibid.*, p. 371.
12. *Ibid.*, p. 407.
13. *Ibid.*

CHAPTER FIVE: SUPERSTAR

1. Woodberry, v. 2, pp. 2–3.
2. *The Letters of Edgar Allan Poe*, v. 1, pp. 235–37 (dated 28 Aug 1843).
3. *The Poe Log*, p. 457.
4. *Ibid.*, p. 473 (printed in "The Home Journal" of 30 October, 1858).
5. *Ibid.*, p. 514.
6. Woodberry, v. 2, p. 137.
7. *The Poe Log*, p. 538.

CHAPTER SIX: A WAY WITH WOMEN

1. Quoted in Griswold's 1850 edition of Poe's works, but considered a forgery by some. Griswold seems to have had great influence over Mrs. Osgood in this last year of her life.
2. *The Poe Log*, p. 547.

3. *Ibid.*, pp. 651–52.
4. Miller, John Carl in *Poe's Helen Remembers,* reprints this letter on p. 178 in an article by John Ingram about Poe that ascribes authorship to an unknown man. *The Poe Log,* p. 669, ascribes it to Mrs. Gove Nichols. The consensus of other sources is that Mrs. Gove Nichols is the writer.
5. *The Poe Log,* p. 675.
6. *The Poe Log,* p. 677.
7. *Poe's Helen Remembers,* p. 120 (written 3 April 1875 by Mrs. Shew Houghton to Ingram).
8. *The Poe Log,* p. 683.
9. *The Letters of Edgar Allan Poe,* v. 2, p. 340.
10. Mrs. Shew Houghton's letter of 28 March 1875 to John Ingram, *The Poe Log,* p. 684.
11. Mrs. Shew Houghton's letter of 23 January 1875 to Ingram, *The Poe Log,* p. 694.
12. *The Letters of Edgar Allan Poe,* v. 2, pp. 350–51.
13. Mrs. Shew Houghton's letter of 23 January 1875 to Ingram, *The Poe Log,* p. 732.
14. *The Letters of Edgar Allan Poe,* v. 2, pp. 351–52.
15. *Ibid.*, v. 2, pp. 372–74.

CHAPTER SEVEN: THE SEARCH
1. *The Poe Log,* p. 754 (letter from Miss Maria J. McIntosh, 15 September 1848).
2. Phillips, Mary E. *Edgar Allan Poe, The Man,* v. 2, p. 1315.
3. Stoddard, Richard Henry. *The Works of Edgar Allan Poe,* v. 1, p. 156.
4. *The Poe Log,* p. 758.
5. *The Letters of Edgar Allan Poe,* v. 2, pp. 391–98.
6. *The Poe Log,* p. 762.
7. *The Letters of Edgar Allan Poe,* v. 2, pp. 400–404.
8. *Poe's Helen Remembers,* letter from Whitman to Ingram 25 October 1875.
9. *The Letters of Edgar Allan Poe,* v. 2, p. 412.
10. *The Poe Log,* pp. 779–80.
11. *Ibid.*, pp. 768–69.
12. *The Letters of Edgar Allan Poe,* v. 2, pp. 414–15.
13. *Ibid.*, v. 2, p. 429.

14. *Ibid.*, v. 2, p. 414–15.
15. *Ibid.*, v. 2, p. 429–32.

CHAPTER EIGHT: THE END OF THE SEARCH
1. Sartain, John, *The Reminiscences of a Very Old Man, 1808–1897*, pp. 207–212.
2. *The Letters of Edgar Allan Poe*, v. 2, p. 452.
3. *The Poe Log*, p. 817.
4. *The Letters of Edgar Allan Poe*, v. 2, pp. 453–55.
5. *Ibid.*, v. 2, pp. 455–56.
6. *The Poe Log*, p. 825–26.
7. *Ibid.*, p. 816.
8. *Ibid.*, p. 821.
9. *Ibid.*, pp. 825–26.
10. *Ibid.*, p. 838.
11. *Ibid.*, p. 840.
12. *Ibid.*, p. 854.
13. *Ibid.*, p. 840.
14. *Ibid.*, p. 848.
15. *Ibid.*, p. 848.

CHAPTER NINE: A GROTESQUE TALE
1. Moran, John J., *A Defense of Edgar Allan Poe*, passim.

BIBLIOGRAPHY

Not all the books in the bibliography are recommended. Many are accessible only in rare and secondhand bookstores or in libraries with old and rare collections; some are badly written and/or inadequately researched; some rant and rave blindly to foster a particular belief; one or two are virtually incomprehensible. The author therefore recommends Wagenknecht, Miller, and Mabbot for their scholarship, readability, and, hopefully, accessibility, and Silverman as the most recent book published to date.

Allen, Hervey. *Israfel: The Life and Times of Edgar Allan Poe.* New York: Farrar & Rinehart, 1926. (2d ed., rev. 1934).

Baudelaire, Charles (translation and preface). *Seven Tales.* Reprint, New York: Schocken Books, 1971.

Campbell, Killis. *The Mind of Poe and Other Studies.* Cambridge, Mass.: Harvard University Press, 1933.

Gill, William. *The Life of Edgar Allan Poe.* New York: C. T. Dillingham, 1877.

Hoffman, Daniel. *Poe Poe Poe Poe Poe Poe Poe.* New York: Doubleday & Co., 1972.

Ingram, John Henry. *Edgar Allan Poe: His Life, Letters, and Opinions.* 1886. Reprint, New York: AMS Press, 1965.

———. *Edgar Allan Poe's Tales.* Vol. 2212, Tauchnitz Edition, Leipzig, 1884.

Lawrence, D. H. *Studies in Classic American Literature*. Thomas Saltzer, Inc., 1923. Reprinted, New York: The Viking Press, 1964.

Mabbott, Thomas Ollive, ed. *Collected Works of Edgar Allan Poe. Volume 1: Poems*. Cambridge, Mass.: Harvard University Press, 1969.

————. Eleanor D. Kewer, and Maureen C. Mabbott, eds. *Collected Works of Edgar Allan Poe, Volume 2: Tales and Sketches*. Cambridge, Mass.: Harvard University Press, 1978.

Mankowitz, Wolf. *The Extraordinary Mr. Poe*. New York: Summit Books, 1978.

Marsden, Simon. *Visions of Poe*. New York: Alfred A. Knopf, 1988.

Miller, John Carl. *Poe's Helen Remembers*. Charlottesville: The University Press of Virginia, 1979.

Moran, John J. *A Defense of Edgar Allan Poe, Life, Character and Dying Declarations of the Poet.* Washington, D.C.: William F. Boogher, 1885.

Ostrom, John Ward, ed. *The Letters of Edgar Allan Poe*. 2 vols. 1948. Reprint, New York: Gordian Press, 1966.

Philips, Mary E. *Edgar Allan Poe, The Man*. Chicago: John C. Winston, 1926.

Poe, Edgar Allan. *Marginalia*. Charlottesville: The University Press of Virginia, 1981.

Quinn, Arthur Hobson. *Edgar Allan Poe: A Critical Biography*. 1941. Reprint, New York: Cooper Square Publishers, 1969.

Regan, Robert, ed. *Poe: A Collection of Critical Essays*. New Jersey: Prentice-Hall, Inc., 1967.

Robertson, John W., M.D. *Edgar Allan Poe: A Psychopathic Study*. New York & London: G. P. Putnam's Sons, 1923.

Sartain, John. *The Reminiscences of a Very Old Man, 1808–1897*. 1899. Reprint, New York and London: Blom, 1969.

Silverman, Kenneth. *Edgar A. Poe, Mournful and Never-Ending Remembrance.* New York: Harper Collins, 1992.

Thomas, Dwight and Jackson, David K. *The Poe Log: A Documentary Life of Edgar Allan Poe 1809–1849.* Boston: G. K. Hall & Co., 1987.

Wagenknecht, Edward. *Edgar Allan Poe, The Man Behind the Legend.* New York: Oxford University Press, 1963.

Walsh, John Evangelist. *Plumes in the Dust: The Love Affair of Edgar Allan Poe and Fanny Osgood.* Chicago: Nelson-Hall, 1980.

Winwar, Frances. *The Haunted Palace, A Life of Edgar Allan Poe.* New York: Harper & Brothers, 1959.

Woodberry, George Edward. *The Life of Edgar Allan Poe, Personal and Literary.* 2 vols. Boston and New York: Houghton Mifflin Co., 1909.

INDEX

ABOUT THE AUTHOR

Madelyn Klein Anderson is a former Army officer and editor of children's books. She holds two graduate degrees: one in occupational therapy from New York University and the other in library science from Pratt Institute in Brooklyn, New York. Ms. Anderson is currently a consultant with the New York City Public Schools and is writing several more books for Franklin Watts.